TYPES OF ENGLISH PIETY

TYPES OF ENGLISH PIETY

BY

R. H. COATS, M.A., B.D.

FORMERLY ELMSLIE SCHOLAR (LONDON), AND
PUSEY AND ELLERTON SCHOLAR (OXFORD)

EDINBURGH: T. & T. CLARK, 38 GEORGE STREET

1912

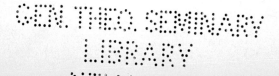

TY... OF

ENGLISH PIETY

R. M. COATS, M.A., D.D.

Printed by
MORRISON & GIBB LIMITED,

FOR

T. & T. CLARK, EDINBURGH.

LONDON: SIMPKIN, MARSHALL, HAMILTON, KENT, AND CO. LIMITED.
NEW YORK: CHARLES SCRIBNER'S SONS.

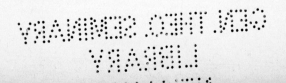

PREFACE

IN the following pages I have endeavoured to interpret, in the light of their ideals, the principal types of piety which have prevailed in England since the Reformation; to study some representative examples of each, in so far as they have found literary expression; to indicate the special weaknesses to which they are severally exposed; and to estimate their respective services to our national religious life.

Parts of the book have already appeared in *The Hibbert Journal, The London Quarterly Review,* and *The Christian World.* By kind permission of the editors, I am enabled to reproduce these articles here in their proper context.

I gladly take this opportunity of expressing my indebtedness to Dr. Rendel Harris, through whose kindness I had the opportunity of first presenting these views to the public in the form of a series of lectures delivered at Woodbrooke; as well as to

Prof. G. Buchanan Gray, D.D., of Mansfield College, Oxford, and Prof. H. Wheeler Robinson, M.A., of Rawdon College, who very generously helped me with criticism and advice while the book was being written.

R. H. COATS.

BIRMINGHAM, *March* 1912.

CONTENTS

——◆——

INTRODUCTION

THE EVANGELICAL TYPE

THE MYSTICAL TYPE

"Καὶ ἤρχοντο πρὸς αὐτὸν πάντοθεν."

MARK i. 45.

"When holy and devout religious men
  Are at their beads, 'tis hard to draw them thence,
So sweet is zealous contemplation."

SHAKESPEARE, *Richard III.*, III. vii.

TYPES OF
ENGLISH PIETY

INTRODUCTION

MANY interesting and pressing questions,
social, historical, ecclesiastical, theological,
and psychological, are suggested by the religious
condition of England at the present day. Can
the bewilderingly varied phenomena of the spiritual
life, now noticeable among us, be regarded as the
manifestations of a few outstanding types? If so,
what are the essential characteristics of each, and
how are they to be distinguished? What are their
roots in history, and through what successive
phases have they passed? Are the different types
of piety in England in any way to be identified
with the different Churches? Is one type to be
found in all the Churches, or does any one Church
include all the types? What are the theological
and philosophical antecedents and implications of
each? Do all run back to the New Testament

itself, and can they equally claim the sanction and approval of Jesus Christ? Why have certain types flourished in the seventeenth century rather than in the eighteenth, and what are the causes leading to the emergence of one particular type at one particular time?

These inquiries are sufficiently interesting in themselves, but they lead to others that are still more fundamental. Do the great classic types of piety which appear in English history arise out of primary distinctions in human nature? Are they in the last resort determined by temperament? We see Newman, for example, after much wandering and unsettlement, gravitating to that type of piety which was most congruous with the fundamental constitution of his mind. Is it so in all cases, and are men Baptists, Catholics, Presbyterians, Methodists, or Unitarians by a kind of pre-established harmony, according as conscience, emotion, intellect, or imagination predominates in their nature? If so, which type builds on conscience, and which on intellect?

A further set of questions arises from the divergence of the types. Why is there no Anglican Bunyan, or Puritan Laud? What exactly is it that makes Bishop Andrewes' *Devotions* so very different from *Grace Abounding* on the one hand,

and the *Theologia Germanica* on the other? For what underlying reasons would it have been impossible that Pusey should ever have worshipped in a Quaker meeting‑house, or George Fox have endured for a moment the pageantries of Rome in Easter week?

Again we may ask ourselves, Is there an English type of piety at all, and does the English character run through all the types? In what ways does ours differ from mediæval piety, or from the piety of the Continent to-day? *Can* there be a national type of piety, as distinct from that which is catholic? If so, which aspects of catholic piety are alien to us, and to which are we particularly attuned?

Finally, do the various types appeal specially to distinct classes of the community? Is there a middle-class type and an upper-class type? How do the types stand related to science, art, and literature, to philanthropic activities and foreign missions? Does any type lean to politics more than another, or to rationalism? If so, how far is the piety chilled or inflamed by the contact? Can it be shown that any one type produces a finer kind of saint than all the others, and more of them? Who are the representative saints in each group? And which type, on the whole, has yielded the best results? Which has accomplished most, in that it has subdued kingdoms, wrought righteousness, stopped the mouths of lions, turned to flight armies of aliens? Which has found the way to the deepest springs of never-failing joy and peace and love?

In pursuing these inquiries it will be well for us, at the outset, to distinguish clearly between piety, theology, and ethics. The relation between doctrine and devotion may be twofold. On the one hand, piety may draw its nourishment from theology, and wing its flight to God by the assistance of the creeds. On the other hand, devotion may be rather the mother of theology than its child. All Christian doctrine rests on an ultimate basis of religious faith, and faith is our own immediate vision and appropriation of the highest. "Mysticism," as Harnack says, "is the presupposition of scholasticism." [1] The heart makes the theologian ere the theologian makes the treatise or the creed, and it is what we first of all feel and know through personal communion with God, as we bow before His throne and devote ourselves to His service, that we afterwards proceed to formulate in a reasoned system of belief. No mere theological acumen, therefore, or dialectic skill, can ever take the place of personal spiritual

---

[1] *History of Dogma* (Eng. trans.), vol. vi. pp. 26, 27.

appropriation, by prayer and faith and love, of those divine realities by which the soul must live.[1]

To the sphere of ethics piety bears quite a different relation. Morals concern themselves with a temporal and mundane good, religion with a good that is transcendent and eternal. The former need not look further than this world. The latter demands for its fulfilment a world beyond the bourne of time and space. Ethics regards God as a means or help necessary for the attainment of righteous conduct. Religion regards Him as Himself the supreme end and goal of the soul's life. No doubt these two are complementary the one to the other. They are the obverse and reverse sides of the same thing, being the godward and manward directions taken by the one spiritual impulse of divine life within the soul. Morality requires religion to sanction its own presuppositions, and to guarantee its own fulfilment and consummation. Religion requires morality for the perfecting of itself, for how can a man love God whom he hath not seen, unless he love his brother whom he hath seen? But in dealing with definitions we must distinguish, and point out that conduct is not piety's immediate or chief concern.

> "Is virtue, then, and piety the same?
> No, piety is more; 'tis virtue's source."[2]

---

[1] Note A.   [2] Young, *Night Thoughts*, viii. 691.

Originally, the word means that natural regard which parents have for their children, or children for their parents. In its spiritual sense, then, piety is the filial affection of the sons of God, "the earnest application of the soul to God, as the only cause and fountain of happiness."[1] It is the effort of man's entire personality to adjust itself to the totality of his spiritual environment, and come to terms of harmony with the supreme overarching and underlying Power, in whom we live and move and have our being.[2] As such, piety has a nobler dignity, a vaster scope, and a more enduring function than morality, which is concerned chiefly with our relations with our fellow-men. Christ's commandment of love to God is ever the first and the greatest commandment, and must take priority over the second, which is but like unto it, and to which, indeed, it gives divine sanction and energizing power. "There is a devotion to God, and God in Christ, which calls for spikenard from secret souls, even at the cost of some obvious service to the poor. . . . There is a life within the life of service and within the fellowship of humanity, which is in the long run the condition of all that is best in human service, and most patient in human pity. Without it enthusiasm for humanity dies. We may love men not wisely but too well in

---

[1] William Law, *Christian Perfection*, chap. xiv.   [2] Note B.

loving them more than God. The soul cannot be
stayed on public service, nor its spiritual ritual
exhausted in beneficence." [1]

Piety, then, concerns itself with our divine relationships, our life in God and with God, our commerce
with the Soul of all reality. It yearns towards that
which is more than socially useful to us, or to others,
in however high a sense, but which has beauty and
value for itself, because of its own infinitude and
divinity. "Suppose that all your objects in life
were realized," John Stuart Mill once asked himself,
" and that all the changes in institutions and opinions,
which you are looking forward to, could be completely effected at this very instant; would this be
a great joy and happiness to you? And an ir-
repressible self-consciousness distinctly answered
'No'!" [2] It is the function of piety to bring us
into touch with those eternal spiritual realities which
are a great joy and happiness to us, in and for themselves, whether the objects of this life be realized or
no. For all religion is based on the assumption that
man not only desires the Infinite and is capable of
apprehending it, but that he is so made as to be
able to find rest and satisfaction in nothing else,
since some part of the Infinite is already in him, not

---

[1] P. T. Forsyth, D.D., *The Person and Place of Christ*, p. 39.
[2] J. S. Mill, *Autobiography*, ed. 1875, pp. 133, 134.

as an alien and foreign element, but as the hidden soul of all his moral being, and even as the necessary condition of his conscious life.

> " Our destiny, our being's heart and home,
> Is with infinitude, and only there ;
> With hope it is, hope that can never die,
> Effort, and expectation, and desire,
> And something evermore about to be." [1]

---

[1] Wordsworth, *Prelude*, vi. 605–608.

reasons of expediency, or unite by their own choice in order to propagate some favourite system of belief. It is not something that has been evolved, devised, or articulated by the will of man. It is the expression of the mind and will of God. That union of God and man which was first consummated in the Incarnation is continued and extended, by means of the Holy Spirit, within the Church, which was founded and commissioned by Christ Himself, if not in scheme and outline at any rate in principle, to be the organ of His life. The Church is the earthly counterpart in time of God's idea of man from all eternity, the Body which has been prepared for Himself by the redeeming Spirit. It is a transcendent unity in Christ before it is a corporate unity in the world. And this organic unity is a necessity of its being. The Church is held together not by ecclesiastical enactments or by legal bonds, but by Christ's own sacramental and indwelling Presence. Through all the grievous lapses and buffetings of its earthly career the Church yet preserves intact the marks of its high origin and divinity. These are the three creeds, the two sacraments, the threefold ministry, and the teaching of the first four centuries. There is no break in its continuity and can be none, since its permanence and universality are those of Him who is the same

ments are valid or efficacious save such as are duly administered by them. The universal priesthood of all believers is indeed recognized and even urged, as well as the sole High Priesthood of Jesus Christ. Yet these do not dispense with the need of an official priesthood, who shall authoritatively mediate the grace of God to the heart, and who shall be commissioned to perform specific acts as the specifically empowered organs of the whole body. Their office is to focus, not to usurp, the functions which belong to all. The grace which they dispense is conceived as a kind of heavenly spiritual life or divine substance, infused into the soul as an antiseptic against sin and a seed of immortality, first in the regenerating waters of Holy Baptism, then in the apostolic laying on of hands in Holy Confirmation, and finally in the life-giving elements of the Holy Communion. It is the crowning privilege and prerogative of the priest that he is the leader and enactor of eucharistic worship, by which the adoring Church becomes identified in time with Christ's eternal act of atoning sacrifice, as consummated both on Calvary and in heaven. The right to perform these functions Christ has committed to the keeping of the clergy in apostolic succession. Their office and order may not another take. Divine grace has chosen and ordained them, that they in their turn may determine the true Church, just as the Church must determine the true Christian.

Episcopal orders, therefore, are essential to the true Church. They are no mere matters of convenience, or expediency of organization, but the very fibres and ligaments themselves by which the Body of Christ, fitly joined together, maketh continual increase unto the edifying of itself in love. And it is not possible for the clergy, however they might wish it, to build the Church of Christ on a fresh site, or base it on some other foundation than that already laid.[1] Whoever, therefore, would become a member of the Body of Christ, must do so not simply by his individual repentance toward God and faith in the Lord Jesus, nor yet by his merely private reception of the influences of divine grace, but by his attitude of due submission to the authority, teaching, and discipline of the one mediating Church, with its valid anointing ministry and its grace of sacraments. Hence it is impossible for any one to be truly joined to Christ and yet to

---

[1] "Revelation is all in all in doctrine, the apostles its sole depository, and ecclesiastical authority its sole sanction. The Divine Voice has spoken once for all, and the only question is about its meaning. . . . When truth can change, its Revelation can change; when human reason can outreason the Omniscient, then may it supersede His work." (J. H. Newman, *The Idea of a University*, p. 223.)

remain voluntarily outside of His visible Church. Christ and the Church are coterminous and co-extensive, and faith in Christ can properly only be generated by, and cultivated within, the corporate society in which He dwells as its abiding life. "The primary and full Bride of Christ never is, nor can be, any individual soul, but only the complete organism of all faithful souls throughout time and space; and the single soul is such a Bride only in so far as it forms an operative constituent of this larger whole."[1] It is not denied that there are good Christians and even saints outside the visible Church, just as there are innumerable grades of sanctity inside it. It is even likely that there may be many without who are immeasurably nearer Christ than many who are within, for it is not possible, in this imperfect world, to draw a perfectly accurate line of demarcation between those who belong to the true Church and those who do not. Still less is it possible to say that in all cases the formal and spiritual boundaries, the areas of Church and Kingdom, exactly coincide. Nevertheless they are essentially and ideally identical, and this identity is to be affirmed through all present conflicts and seeming contradictions and uncharitableness, in the interests of that final settle-

[1] Fr. von Hügel, *The Mystical Element in Religion*, vol. ii. p. 356.

ment which shall openly establish it beyond all cavilling. If any one, therefore, chooses to reject or dispense with the appointed institutions of the Church, thinking to respond of himself, directly, to the grace and mercy of God in Christ, and so become, as it were, a Christian first and a Church member afterwards, his is an emasculated and insufficient faith, truncated and incomplete, and of very doubtful validity for the saving of the soul.[1] He may enjoy irregular and uncovenanted mercies. But he has violated a law of the Church's life, and has not yet risen to the height of his privileges and responsibilities. Not till he enters the one Body can he share to the full in the blessed redeeming energies of the Eternal Sacrifice.

The scope of the present work does not admit of our studying the sacerdotal conception of Christianity as it reaches its most perfect and consistent form in Roman Catholicism. It is sufficient that we find it embedded in the formularies, and expressed also in the worship, of the Anglican Church, in a way which faithfully reflects the English character, both in its weakness and in its strength. There is,

---

[1] "To the thought of Paul, the act of faith in the individual which brings him within the range of justification is inseparably connected with its ratification in baptism. . . . Justification is normally mediated through the Church." (Sanday and Headlam, *Commentary on Romans*, p. 123.)

in the Anglican standards of faith and worship, a remarkable sanity and breadth, a sobriety, a moderation, a wholesome love of compromise, and a hatred of extremes.   According to a quaint figure much loved of the older divines, the Church of England is placed, like our Lord, between two thieves, with this difference that in her case *both* of them are impenitent.   On the one hand is Calvin of Geneva, but he is too much of a preacher.[1]   On the other the Pope of Rome, but he is too much of a priest. The true mean is to be found somewhere between the lake and the seven hills.   Romanism is too trivial and arrogant for her liking, while Puritanism spells humbug and savours too much of cant.   The former exaggerates the importance of the external in religion, while the latter, with equal excess, disdains it.   The true Church of Christ will abjure, if she be wise, the superstitious mummery of the one and the fanatical enthusiasm of the other; and her grave and chaste ritual will eschew both the tawdriness of the mass and the naked plainness of the conventicle, as repugnant alike to decency and order and reverence and good taste.

It is probable that in thus characteristically

---

[1] " Resort to sermons, but to prayers most ;
       Praying's the end of preaching."
                          GEORGE HERBERT, *The Church Porch*.

moulding the national Church so as to reflect the national mind and heart, Englishmen have acted, perhaps unconsciously, rather as practical men and statesmen than as theologians. The typical churchman of English history, whether he may have lived in Tudor, Stuart, or Hanoverian times, has seldom been overcurious to inquire whether the principles of the Dissenters or Roman Catholics were theoretically more logical, thoroughgoing, and consistent than his own. It was enough that the former conducted themselves like rebels, in his opinion, and the latter like foreigners, and that he felt an instinctive dread and suspicion of them both, as likely, between them, to jeopardize the stability of the constitution. According to his view of the matter, the Church of Christ in England should exclude nothing and include everything that was soundly and characteristically national. It must be insular and yet catholic, but the former first. It must be primitive and apostolic, yet modern and reformed. It must speak with authority, yet leave plenty of latitude for private judgment. It must build on the Scripture, yet appeal to reason. It must be supernatural in its claims, yet derive its authority from the State. Its articles must be exclusive, and yet comprehensive too. Is the result a compromise? Never mind that, if it works well. The Church of

2

and the saints made perfect, is kept constantly before the imagination of the devout believer. The Church is never suffered to forget her prototype in the heavens, where in God's unseen temple everything cries glory, and elders and living creatures swing their golden censers before the throne. It is no small part of the spell of Anglican worship that it impresses on the mind the intimate connection of every village sanctuary with that Church which is invisible and eternal in the heavens, in which a choir of celestial voices chant the unwearied hymn, Holy, Holy, Holy, to the Lamb that was slain, and to Him that sitteth on the throne, for ever and ever.

When a Church of England service is well rendered, dull indeed must be the soul that would fail to worship. The stateliest architecture, the sweetest and most solemn music, the chastest language, the goodliest vestments, the most seemly postures, and the most suggestive ceremonies are all brought into requisition to assist the sluggish soul in its flight toward God. Surely, if a man's spirit could take wing above the earth, it would be under these conditions. The eye is wooed heavenwards by soaring columns or by storied glass. The ear is won by melodies that either melt to penitence or stir to praise. The statues on the walls or the brasses beneath the feet speak of the sainted dead, and beckon to those good things whereto they have attained. Even the reverberating echoes and the restful shade invite to tranquil thoughts and solemn vows.

A characteristic feature of sacerdotal worship is its whole-hearted delight in symbolism and love of art. This arises naturally from its sacramental principle. The evangelical type of piety inclines to an ethical dualism in religion, and is on the whole suspicious of art. Its tendency is to separate the spiritual from the material, to dwell rather on the inward than on the outward, and to look on the sacraments of the Church as no more than suggestive symbols of the divine. The mystical type goes even farther in this direction and drifts towards a vague formlessness of emotion, which would reject everything that is outward, and dispense with the need of sacraments altogether. A sacerdotal Church of necessity stoutly opposes itself to both these tendencies. In contradistinction to mysticism it disparages mere subjective feeling, emphasizes the importance of the objective, the definite, the dogmatic, as a basis for our faith, and insists with the poet that

> " Eternal form shall still divide
> The eternal soul from all beside." [1]

On the other hand it differs from most forms of

[1] Tennyson, *In Memoriam*, xlvii.

evangelicalism in affirming that the sacraments do not merely suggest or express spiritual realities, but positively embody and convey them, as they could not be conveyed by any other mode.   As in the sacrament of all true art, substance and form are here complementary and inseparable.   The outward does not simply represent the inward.   It *is* the inward, clothed in the only form in which it is possible for us to apprehend it by our earthly faculties.   Matter is not the antithesis of spirit, but its home and living garment, something used to shadow forth the highest truths, and even to become the dwelling-place of that divine Being who giveth to spiritual realities a body, even as it pleaseth Him.   This tendency finds its warrant and consummation in the sublime mystery of the Incarnation, which is the Word made Flesh, spirit finding speech by taking form, and, when used with due restraint, it leads to much that is most characteristic and inspiring in sacerdotal worship.   It is not enough, according to this view, that the Bride of the Most High should be all glorious within.   It is meet and right that her clothing should be of wrought gold.   Her garments must smell of myrrh, aloes, and cassia, if God is to anoint her with the oil of gladness above her fellows.[1]

[1] How strongly the characteristic worship of sacerdotal piety appealed to Ruskin, even in his earlier and more evangelical days,

Hence the fond and luxuriating fancy with which, in this type of piety, art loves to decorate the shrine of the Most High.   Bezaleel and Aholiab are called in to assist Aaron in the worship of the temple. That vine, with its creeping tendrils, is to remind us of Him in whom we must be grafted as living branches if we are to bear fruit unto holiness and eternal life.   That lily, so white and spotless and rich in fragrance, does it not tell of the Madonna, the innocence and grace of the Mother-Maid ?   The North reminds us of Lucifer (Isa. xiv. 13) and the Gentiles, the East of Paradise and the resurrection glory.   Where blue sky can be represented, it speaks of Mary's purity or the illimitable vault of the love of God; and if a star can be made to shine somewhere, it will serve to guide our thoughts, if we

may be judged from the following lines written after a visit to Rouen Cathedral in 1848.   " I felt convinced that, freed from abuses, this *mode* of service was the right one, and that if bishops were bishops indeed, and priests were priests indeed—and if the doctrines of purgatory and bought absolution, of Mariolatry, and of the vicariousness of the Pope—above all, if dishonesty and doing evil that good might come and the doctrine of salvation by works were cast out of the Church, and the Bible were made free to the people—that all these proud pillars and painted casements, all these burning lamps and smoking censers, all these united voices and solemn organ peals had their right and holy use in this their service, and that all these white robed priests and young troops of novice and chorister could be, and ought to be, devoted to their lofty duties, and separated from the common world without offence, yea, and with high honour, before God."   (E. T. Cook, *The Life of Ruskin*, vol. i. p. 228.)

are wise, to the lowly cot of Bethlehem, where the young Child lay. So also with the endless uses that can be made of the nails, the wooden cross, the crown of thorns, the circle, the triangle, the A and the Ω, the I.H.S. Are not even the numerals sacred and symbolical, three for the triune God, five for the wounds of Christ, seven for the gifts of the Spirit or the number of deadly sins? Finally, the array of banners and of candles, the standing at the reading of the Gospel, the turning eastwards for the Creed, the use of the sign of the cross, and the bowing at the name of Jesus, all are intended to help our languid and flagging spirits. They are to be regarded, on the one hand, as spiritual good manners, the most seemly and appropriate expression which men can render of the debt of love, gratitude, and adoration which we owe to Almighty God, and, on the other hand, as the appeals of the living Christ within the veil, who would fain give wings to our faith and bid it rise.[1]

The crowning act of worship in this sacerdotal system is, of course, the supreme offering of the Holy Eucharist, in which God's love to man and man's to God are expressed in a way that transcends all human language. This is indeed the inner shrine and holy of holies of the soul's fellowship with God.

[1] Note D.

" will as much as in them lieth know all things that God commandeth, but especially the duties of service which they owe to God. As for his dark and hidden works, they prefer as becometh them in such cases simplicity of faith before that knowledge, which, curiously sifting what it should adore, and disputing too boldly of that which the wit of man cannot search, chilleth for the most part all warmth of zeal, and bringeth soundness of belief many times into great hazard. Let it therefore be sufficient for me presenting myself at the Lord's table to know what there I receive from him, without searching or inquiring of the manner how Christ performeth his promise; let disputes and questions, enemies to piety, abatements of true devotion, and hitherto in this cause but over patiently heard, let them take their rest; let curious and sharp-witted men beat their heads about what questions themselves will, the very letter of the word of Christ giveth plain security, that these mysteries do as nails fasten us to his very Cross, that by them we draw out, as touching efficacy, force, and virtue, even the blood of his gored side, in the wounds of our Redeemer we there dip our tongues, we are dyed red both within and without, our hunger is satisfied and our thirst for ever quenched; they are things wonderful which he feeleth, great which he seeth, and unheard

serpentine, porphyry, and chalcedon; the shining walls, veined with the richest marbles and studded with gems; the roof of the nave, carved with foliage and roses overlaid with gold; the distant walls and chambers of imagery, dim with incense, through which shone out, scarcely veiled, the statues and tombs, the paintings and crucifixes and altars with their glimmering lights;—all settled down, so to speak, upon Inglesant's soul with a perception of subdued splendour which hushed the spirit into a silent feeling which was partly rest and partly awe.

"But when, having traversed the length of the nave without uttering a word, he passed from under the gilded roofs, and the spacious dome, lofty as a firmament, expanded itself above him in the sky, covered with tracery of the celestial glories and brilliant with mosaic and stars of gold; when, opening on all sides to the wide transepts, the limitless pavement stretched away beyond the reach of sense; when beneath this vast work and finished effort of man's devotion, he saw the high altar, brilliant with lights, surmounted and enthroned by its panoply of clustering columns and towering cross; when, all around him, he was conscious of the hush and calmness of worship, and felt in his inmost being the sense of vastness, of splendour, and of awe;—he may be pardoned if, kneeling upon the polished

floor, he conceived for the moment that this was
the house of God, and that the gate of heaven was
here.

.   .   .   .

   "Inglesant passed up the church towards the
high altar before which he knelt : and as he did so,
a procession, carrying the Sacrament, entered by
another door and advanced to the altar upon
which it was again deposited. The low melancholy
miserere—half entreating, half desponding—spoke
to the heart of man a language like its own ; and
as the theme was taken up by one of the organs,
the builder's art and the musician's melted into
one, in tier after tier of carved imagery, in wave
after wave of mystic sound. All conscious thought
and striving seemed to fade from the heart, and
before the altar and amid the swell of sound the
soul lost itself and lay silent and passive in the
Eternal Love."[1]

   It is not surprising that a worshipper accustomed
to this kind of devotion, with its rich and multifarious sensuous appeal, should regard with infinite
pity and even scorn the bare and jejune worship
of Evangelical Protestantism.[2] How naked and
graceless and irreverent it must appear ! The High

---

[1] J. H. Shorthouse, *John Inglesant*, chaps. xxiv. and xxxv.
[2] Note E.

Churchman turns shivering from such profanities, having the desire, not to be unclothed, but to be clothed upon, wrapt round about with all that may be seemly and suggestive of the divine. He shrinks from the unfettered licence of a " free " worship, and craves the grave restraint, the ordered chastened beauty of a stately ritual. Above all, he demands that the incomparable sacrifice of the Cross shall be set forth visibly, and with such enriching accompaniments as are its due. Yes, George Meredith, who has said the last word on so many things, has truly divined the heart of this type of piety in the words of one of his characters. "Stir us to the depths and we are poor soupy stuff. For estimable language and the preservation of self-respect in prostration we want ritual, ceremonial elevation of the visible object for the soul's adoring through the eye. So may we escape our foul and empty selves. It is natural to worship, and only the Catholics can prostrate themselves with dignity. . . . I left him with a Catholic lord for comforter, who regards my prescript of the study of Nature, when we're in grief, as about the same as an offer of a dish of cold boiled greens. Silver and ivory images are more consoling." [1]

---

[1] George Meredith, *The Amazing Marriage*, chaps. xxxviii. and xl.

II

Among the crowd of dissolute and fawning time-servers who for the most part made up the court of King James the First, it is pleasing to find so erudite and saintly a figure as that of LANCELOT ANDREWES, bishop successively of Chichester, of Ely, and of Winchester. He appears before us, in the chronicles of the time, in many aspects. Now we see him as a man so learned that Bacon himself was well content to submit to him the proofs of his greatest work;[1] and now as one so human withal, that Casaubon was glad to entreat his company at Stourbridge Fair, and beg that he would shut up his books and come and shoot a buck in Downham Park. Anon he is walking to Chiswick for recreation, with "a brace of young fry" from Westminster School, and "beguiling that wayfaring leisure by filling their narrow vessels with a funnel." Anon he is strolling through the aisles of St. Paul's Cathedral, to impart spiritual counsel and comfort to the distressed. The good man would sometimes warm the heart of his chaplains when they preached by asking them, at the close, if they would favour him with a perusal of

---

[1] Isaacson speaks of his "profundity and abyss of learning" (*Life*, p. xxvi); and Fuller says "the world wanted learning to know how learned this man was." (*Church History*, xi. i. 46.)

the manuscript from which they had discoursed, and he encouraged them still more by professing, without shame, that " if he preached twice on a Sunday at St. Giles, he prated once."

Fuller tells us that his gravity of manner greatly awed King James, "who refrained from that mirth and liberty, in the presence of this prelate, which otherwise he assumed to himself." But it seems this awe and gravity were sometimes relaxed, for we read of Andrewes having entertained the King at Farnham Castle, where in the space of three days he spent on him the sum of £3000, "to the extraordinary contentment of his majesty and the admiration of all his followers." James, indeed, made good use of his episcopal courtier,[1] and employed him, as the mood was on him, to answer Cardinal Bellarmine, or to accompany him to Scotland, or to save his face in the scandalous affair of the Earl of Essex. But the true Andrewes, the Andrewes who has come down the centuries and appeals to us to-day, is not Andrewes the hospitable prelate, nor Andrewes the learned controversialist, nor even Andrewes the mighty hunter before the Lord, but Andrewes the humble-minded

---

[1] " The most learned King James . . . selected him, as his choicest piece, to vindicate his regality against foul-mouthed adversaries." (Isaacson, *Life*, p. ix.)

Christian saint, as, leaving behind him the distractions of high place and the vexations of a corrupt court, and turning his back on James, Bacon, Bellarmine and everybody else, he retires to his closet and shuts to the door, and spends "a great part of five hours every day in prayer,"[1] pouring out his soul in a little book of devotions which before the end was to be "slubbered with pious hands, and watered with penitential tears."[2]

Andrewes was fitted in many ways to be a typical representative of Anglican piety. He came at a time when the Prayer Book had recently been compiled, and had distilled into itself the quintessence of all the liturgies of the historic Church. The Church of England was in a state of pristine purity, having emerged from that slovenly condition of worldliness and neglect into which it had been allowed to fall during the reign of Elizabeth. Hooker had just completed his monumental work, in which he had walked about Zion, and gone round about her, told the towers thereof, marked well her bulwarks, considered her palaces, to tell it once for all to the generations following. Laud, too, was beginning to rise into prominence, stemming the tide of Puritanism and robing the Church once

---

[1] Buckeridge, Funeral Sermon in *Works*, vol. v. p. 296.
[2] Richard Drake, Preface to the *Devotions*, ed. 1648.

3

more in her goodly garments. It was the age of Shakespeare and Drake and Raleigh, when a strong tide of patriotism was running, and the fear of Roman supremacy, as it had been successively embodied in Mary Queen of Scots, in Cardinal Allen, in Philip II. of Spain, and in Guy Fawkes, had been done away. It was the age, too, of the Authorized Version of the Bible, when the wells of our national speech were pure and undefiled. And in the courage and confidence of the nation the Church of England shared. It only wanted a man of great learning and distinguished piety, who should follow up the work of Hooker, prove that the Church, now securely Protestant, was also Catholic, and turn the hearts of her children to the Fathers, and away from Calvin.

The man for such a work was Bishop Andrewes. His encyclopædic learning, his knowledge of fifteen languages,[1] his minute familiarity with the Scriptures, his reverence for antiquity and tradition, his love of nature,[2] and of ceremony,[3] his first hand acquaint-

---

[1] Buckeridge, Funeral Sermon in *Works*, vol. v. p. 291.

[2] "He would often profess that to observe the grass, herbs, corn, trees, cattle, earth, waters, heavens, any of the creatures, and to contemplate their natures, orders, qualities, virtues, uses, etc., was ever to him the greatest mirth, content, and recreation that could be." (Isaacson, *Life*, p. vi.)

[3] "His chapel was so decently and reverently adorned, and God served there with so holy and reverent behaviour, that some that

ance with the secrets of the human heart,[1] peculiarly
fitted him to embody the best ideals of Anglican
devotion.　He is the expression, says one of his
biographers, of " the true tone and character which
the Church of England aims at forming in her
children, largeness of sympathy, self-restraint, sober-
ness, fervour, the spirit of continuous but not un-
hopeful penitence." [2]

It is this which makes the perusal of the *Preces
Privatae* the best substitute, in secret, for a cathedral
service.　It has the same chaste majesty and ordered
beauty; the same gradual preparation and raising
of the soul from the level of the world to the
loftiest heights of meditation; the same well-
thought-out marshalling of our spiritual needs
according to their related parts; the same abase-
ment for sin, and adoring, exultant wonder at the
grace of Christ; the same personal note of direct
and individual access to the Father, combined with
the sense of being at one with the Holy Catholic
Church throughout the world.　The *Preces Privatae*
are the compilation of one who has always in his
public devotions sought to be clothed upon and

had been there were so taken with it that they desired to end their
days in the Bishop of Ely's Chapel." (Isaacson, *Life*, p. xiii.)

[1] "He was a man deeply seen in all cases of conscience."
(*Ibid*. p. vii.)

[2] R. L. Ottley, *Lancelot Andrewes*, p. 180.

upheld by the appointments of the Church, who has loved to feel that the Lord was round about him, as the mountains are round about Jerusalem, in all goodly ceremonial and seemly ritual, and who in his private devotions would fain call upon the same aids and suggestions to his spirit. His book of prayers is a personal transcript of the offices of the Church, and registers afresh in the closet those influences which have streamed upon him in the cathedral. There is nothing casual in his petitions or slipshod in his praises. His words are a mosaic of the finest spiritual outpourings of prophet, psalmist, apostle and evangelist, with here and there a gem from the ancient liturgies. Andrewes draws his treasures from all sources, precious things from the heavens above and from the depth that coucheth beneath. The Thirty-Nine Articles and the Creeds drop fatness, and lo ! wild honey is found to be concealed even in the rocky crevices of the *Quicunque Vult*.

What impresses one most in Andrewes' *Devotions* is his carefully methodical survey of the whole ground. The division of the prayers according to the days of the week ; the association of each with an opening meditation on one of God's wonders in the creation of the world ; the scrupulous care with which he differentiates prayer into adoration, supplication, confession, thanksgiving; the exhaustive enumeration of sins to be deplored and graces to be desired; the copiousness and conciseness of his Scriptural phraseology; the minute dwelling on the elements of our human nature, or on the doctrines of the Church, with the devotions which these severally suggest—how painstaking, and orderly, and comprehensive it all is!

Especially is this particularity and definiteness noticeable in his intercessions. These are no vague generalizations, but patient recollections of all who have a claim on him, from whatever cause. His household and benefactors are studiously remembered. He includes in his review all sorts and conditions of men, from the king on his throne and the members of his court, to farmers, graziers, tradesmen, mechanics, artizans. Virgins and voyagers are not forgotten, nor are those "in bitter servitude in mines and galleys." He prays for the peace of Jerusalem and the prosperity of Zion. He prays, too, for propitious weather and fruitful seasons. Over all one is reminded of angels and archangels, thrones, dominations, princedoms, powers. It is a vast well-ordered universe into which the soul is led. Andrewes passes nothing over, gives nothing undue prominence, and never loses sight of the distinctions between high and low, king and subject, rich and

poor. All are gathered with him into the one
temple, and are given their appropriate pleadings
before the throne of grace.

There are times when the writer's words throb
and quiver, and behind the printed page we seem
almost to see that soiled original manuscript which
he moistened with his tears. The *Devotions* were
not intended for publication, and when Andrewes
lays bare before God the red chasm of his sin, or
asks for " a dropping eye," or pleads that " if he
may not weep as bitterly as Peter or as plentifully
as Jeremiah," God would at least give him " one or
two little tears " to put into His bottle, we can only
bow reverently at so much strong wrestling and
poignant spiritual anguish.

But in the main the *Devotions* breathe an
atmosphere of tranquil catholicity and chastened
calm. Andrewes has all the Anglican virtues of
restraint, moderation, and love of order. He is
importunate and yet measured, personal yet catholic
too. He avoids excessive individuality in his
approach to God, and has no liking for a piety of
unregulated spontaneity or disjointed licence.[1] He
is content to put himself to school with the great
classical examples of the piety of the past, and with

[1] Cf. Buckeridge, " He ever misliked often and loose preaching,
without study of antiquity." (*Works*, vol. v. p. 295.)

of the English Church may thus be said to have been linked heart to heart, and we may be pardoned if we make use of this epistolary connection in passing from one to the other. The two had much in common. Each had the honour to be consulted by Lord Bacon about his writings, before they were submitted to the public. Each won the favour of King James, championed his cause, and followed in his court. Andrewes, being a great prelate, was permitted to draw much nearer to that distinguished luminary, and somewhat singed his wings in the royal flame. Herbert had the wisdom to revolve at a greater distance, and after a brief taste of court life, was content to live and die in the obscurity of a country parsonage. But though they thus represent very different phases of the Church life of the time, both were one in their passion of love and loyalty to the Church itself. If Andrewes wove the Prayer Book and the Scriptures into a well-designed tapestry of devotion, Herbert took up his viol and his lute and tuned them into song. He is the sweet singer of our English Israel, the poet of the comeliness and artistic refinement of the Anglican ritual, the spirit of Laud versified. The grave sweet symbolism of the Church easily won his soul from the allurements of the court and the anarchy of a selfish life. Cheerfully he abjured Venus for the

Herbert looked for his inspiration to sources from which the strict Puritan would have turned in revolt, and Coleridge was quite right when he said that the appreciative reader of *The Temple* must be "an affectionate and dutiful child of the Church, and from habit, conviction, or a constitutional predisposition to ceremoniousness in piety as in manners, find her forms and ordinances aids to religion, not sources of formality."[1] To Herbert there must be a *beauty* of holiness, a beauty outward and visible, something to elicit, regulate, and sustain the affections of the soul. Church order is to him as truly a divine order as the music of the spheres, of which, indeed, it is the earthly counterpart. And to be identified with this divine order, as it has been determined and approved by apostles, saints, and martyrs, to fulfil all it requires with grace and gladness, is to be made partaker of the highest bliss that can be given to the soul. Herbert's happiness is that of a man who has turned God's laws into lyrics, His statutes into songs, and who has learned to regulate his life by the church bell. There are moods when he would gladly address his vows to Holy Mary, or crave the special aid of saints and angels, but Mother Church forbids, and to her wise judgment he patiently submits. Herbert believes

---

[1] Introduction to the Notes on Herbert's *Poems* (Pickering).

with his whole soul that no employment is so honourable as the service of the altar of the King of kings,
and that no man on earth is so to be envied as the
country parish priest of the Church of England.
The following hymn of love to *The British Church*
may be taken as typical of his whole attitude :—

> "I joy, deare Mother, when I view
> Thy perfect lineaments, and hue
>   Both sweet and bright.
>
> Beautie in thee takes up her place,
> And dates her letters from thy face,
>   When she doth write.
>
> A fine aspect in fit array,
> Neither too mean, nor yet too gay,
>   Shows who is best.
>
> Outlandish looks may not compare :
> For all they either painted are,
>   Or else undrest.
>
> She on the hills, which wantonly
> Allureth all, in hope to be
>   By her preferr'd,
>
> Hath kiss'd so long her painted shrines,
> That ev'n her face by kissing shines,
>   For her reward.
>
> She in the valley is so shie
> Of dressing, that her hair doth lie
>   About her eares :
>
> While she avoids her neighbour's pride,
> She wholly goes on th' other side,
>   And nothing wears.

> But dearest Mother, (what those misse)
> The mean thy praise and glorie is,
>   And long may be.
>
> Blessed be God, whose love it was
> To double moat thee with his grace,
>   And none but thee."

Herbert's was not the piety which sees God across a gulf, and cries to Him out of the awful pit and from the miry clay. There is little in him of the terrors of the Lord, or the tortures and self-accusations of a guilty conscience. To speak of these things in such language as Andrewes or Bunyan employed would be to sin against poetic feeling and good taste. The truth is that Herbert's God was Himself too much of a poet to be really terrible. He was the amiable heavenly prototype of the Country Parson himself, a Being ever ready to " throw away his rod," and who only inflicted on man such sorrow as was needful to " toss him to His breast." To the grace of such a God, and the mystery of His sufferings in Christ the soul of Herbert responded with a love that never spent itself, and a wonder that never tired. Well might Baxter say of him that next to the Scripture poems there were " none so savoury " as those of Herbert. " He speaks to God like a man that really believeth in God, and whose business in the world is most with God. Heart work and heaven work make up his book." [1]

His book, yes, and not less so his life. We watch this quondam wit and courtier changing his sword and silk clothes for a canonical coat, and showing himself ready to dispense even with that when charity required it, as on the day when he " helped a poor man with a poorer horse, that was fallen under his load," on the way to Salisbury ; or we see him going out and in among his flock " praising God not so much that he is able as that he is willing to be generous in acts of charity," and gathering his family together twice a day to offer prayers, " which were always of a set form and not long"; or we overhear him solacing himself with music on his deathbed, and so singing himself into the presence of the angels, and we love George Herbert, and Walton who so quaintly tells us of him, and thank God that England has so hallowed a spot of ground as Bemerton Parish. Herbert is perhaps the finest example in our history of that gentle and unassuming type of piety which has been so abundantly delineated in our English literature. It appears in various representatives, such as Chaucer's Poure Persoun, in Goldsmith's Vicar of Wakefield, in Sir Roger de Coverley's chaplain, in Crabbe's Parish

---

[1] Preface to *Poetical Fragments.*

Priest, and in that most lovable of simpletons, Parson Adams. The features of these may vary, but the type is constant. It is that of the faithful, unambitious country clergyman, who moves in a peaceful atmosphere of cultured godliness and unaffected love to his fellow-men. Of such a type Herbert was the living embodiment, and the book which he has written for us is a true and worthy casket of his spirit, and of the spirit of that institution which he loved.

It is one of the glories of England that it is rich in an ancient heritage of country churches. We come upon them in summer walks, embosomed in stately elms, and girt with a quiet border of mossy graves. And we always find it good to turn aside from the dusty roadway to their grateful shade, and to open our souls to the influence of their chaste and seemly altars, their chimes, their sleeping tombs. At such times, if we would enter into the spirit of these tranquil shrines, know the secret of their spell, taste their simple charm, and realize what they stand for in our English life, we cannot do better than take from our pocket a copy of Herbert's *Temple*, and, with a heart purged from all vanity and worldly care, read ourselves prayerfully into the spirit of their quaint and courtly lines.

For our last illustration of the sacerdotal type of

piety we turn to the devout prophet and champion
of the Tractarian Movement, JOHN KEBLE.   At first
sight it might seem that Keble should properly be
grouped with the Nature Mystics, so steeped is he
in the spirit of Wordsworth, and so well has he
learned from him the art of holding fellowship with
the highest by means of "the witchery that is in
the soft blue sky," or the humblest flowers that
blow by the wayside.   By the quiet watercourses
of Fairford and Coln St. Aldwyn's, Keble walked
with God.   The rainbow, the snowdrop, the willow,
the robin redbreast gave him sacramental thoughts.
They were outward visible signs of an inward invisible grace.[1]   Newman was impressed with this,
and tells us that the main intellectual truth which
Keble brought home to him was "what may be
called, in the large sense of the word, the sacramental system, that is, the doctrine that material
phenomena are both the types and the instruments
of real things unseen."[2]   Indeed, Keble expressly
defended this position in No. 89 of the *Tracts for
the Times*, and maintained that the works of God
were "so many tokens from the Almighty to assure

[1] For Keble's references to Nature in *The Christian Year*, see
especially the poems allotted to the Fourth Sunday in Advent, to
Septuagesima Sunday, and to the Fourth and Twentieth Sundays
after Trinity.

[2] *Apologia*, p. 18.

us of some spiritual fact or other, which it concerns us to know." [1]

Yet Nature was no more than the porch to that temple of the soul in which Keble most intimately worshipped. The true home of his devotion was the Catholic Church. In one of his poems [2] he affirms that God is not so near to us in "twilight stars on high," or in "moist flowers at even," as He is in a babe that has just been sprinkled at the Church font. This is not merely an illustration of Keble's well-known love for the sweetness and innocence of children. It represents his consistent attitude on the doctrines of grace. Near though God may be in nature, He is nearer far in the sacraments. All other symbolism, of nature or of art, is but a faint adumbration of the symbolism of the Church. "What the Virgin Mother was to the great painters of Italy the Anglican or Elizabethan Church became to him, immaculate in conception, peerless in beauty, resplendent with every grace, a living personality to be loved and wooed, a divine impersonation to be adored and hymned." [3] To Keble Baptismal Regeneration and the Real Presence of Christ in the Eucharist were the glory and crown of the Christian faith. The latter, indeed,

[1] W. Lock, *Life of Keble*, p. 100.   [2] "Holy Baptism."
[3] Sir J. Stephen, *Essays in Ecclesiastical Biography*, p. 448.

summed up in itself the entire creed. " By receiving His creatures of bread and wine, we acknowledge Him Creator of heaven and earth, against all sorts of Manicheans; receiving Christ's body is confessing His Incarnation, adoring it, His Divinity; it is the memorial of His death, and the participation in that sacrifice which supposes Him raised and ascended into heaven; it is the obeying of His commandment so to show forth His death till He come; it is the drinking into the one Spirit; it is the partaking of that one Bread which makes us one Body, the Holy Catholic Church; it is the Communion of Saints; it is the Blood shed for the remission of sins; it is the last Adam coming to be a quickening spirit to seal us for the Resurrection of the Body and the Life Everlasting."[1]   Keble, indeed, in his best verse distils the pure spirit of that master whom he edited and whom he chiefly honoured, Richard Hooker. Reason, nature, scripture, creeds, traditions, all are made welcome and all are utilized in his poetic art. But all are valued only so far as they lead up to the altar at last, and leave us prostrate in adoration before that mingling of mystery and revelation which is symbolized by the Cross.

There are two distinct notes in Keble's churchmanship, the blast of the trumpet and the crooning of

[1] Quoted by W. Lock, *Life of Keble*, p. 164.

4

men back to this way of life, even though it might
be sharp and dusty to the feet, a strait and narrow
way all hedged with briers, Keble swept his apostolic
lyre with passion and with scorn.

> "One only Way to Life;
>   One Faith, delivered once for all;
> One holy Band, endowed with Heaven's high call;
>   One earnest, endless strife;—
> This is the Church th' Eternal framed of old.
>
>   Smooth open ways, good store;
>   A Creed for every clime and age,
> By Mammon's touch new moulded o'er and o'er;
>   No cross, no war to wage;—
> This is the Church our earth-dimmed eyes behold.
>
>   But ways must have an end,
>   Creeds undergo the trial flame,
> Nor with th' impure the Saints for ever blend,
>   Heaven's glory with our shame:
> Think on that hour, and choose 'twixt soft and bold."[1]

Keble wrote these lines with the old Stuart and
Nonjuring family traditions coursing hot within his
blood, and in them the true genius of the Church of
England speaks out It is a piety which believes
unflinchingly that peace and joy are to be found
only in self-discipline and sobriety and obedience to
ancient rule, and that the authority and mysteries
of the faith once for all delivered to the saints shall
withstand to the end of time every rising flood of

[1] *Lyra Apostolica*, "The One Way."

fanaticism or error. It is vain for human reason to lift up her proud waves against that Church of God which is the pillar and ground of the truth, and which has its foundations firm in the Rock of Ages.

But there is quite another note in Keble, a tender and wooing note. *The Christian Year*, he himself tells us, was written "to promote a sober standard of feeling in matters of practical religion," and to exhibit the "soothing tendency of the Prayer Book." In this he has entirely succeeded. There are plenty of stern pieces in the volume, and it closes on a note of holy fear. Yet all the tenderer emotions which the liturgy awakes, moods of chastened penitence, of longing for restoration, of trust in the mercy of God, and intense personal love to Jesus Christ, are here enshrined in pages of cheerful and tranquil beauty. Keble, like the others whom we have been studying, has no desire to transcend the Prayer Book, or to set it aside in the interests of a supposed more immediate access to the throne of grace. To roam within its borders is liberty enough, the kind of liberty which a tired man feels within the four walls of his home. It is the virtue of Keble that he gives one this warm home feeling towards the ordinances of the Church. He has made multitudes realize that the love of God and the love of the Church may be one and the same love, and that there are no such joys as those which well up quietly in the atmosphere she provides. It must of course be remembered that the man who wrote " Sun of my soul! Thou Saviour dear," has warmed the hearts of thousands who have no sympathy whatever with the High Church doctrines he professed. Yet these were the doctrines that made him what he was. And surely in him wisdom is justified of her children. "If any poems can be found to enliven in dejection, to comfort in anxiety, to cool the oversanguine, to refresh the weary and to awe the worldly, to instil resignation into the impatient, and calmness into the fearful and agitated, they are these."[1]

III

Having seen something of the glories and excellences of this type of piety, we may now, with all gratitude and affection, and with what impartiality we possess, proceed to an examination of its defects. In doing so it may be well at the outset to remember that the weaknesses which attach themselves to this as to every other type of piety are not necessarily inherent in it. The perversions and abuses which

[1] J. H. Newman, *Essays*, vol. ii. p. 441.

are inseparably bound up with every earthly system its own pure ideal and typical examples themselves most unsparingly condemn. *Corruptio optimi pessima* is a familiar Latin proverb which we should do well to keep in mind in this connection. Every system is entitled to be judged by its spiritual ideal rather than by its poor and imperfect concrete embodiment and performance. Any strictures, therefore, which may here or elsewhere in this book be passed upon a particular type of piety are to be regarded as a criticism of its abuses and not as a condemnation of itself.

The first defect observable in sacerdotal piety will already have become manifest in our study of the poet Keble, a certain exclusive and intolerant spirit of partizanship, and a slowness to recognize the presence of God save in stereotyped channels and appointed modes. "The opinion that there can be good men in all parties is a bad doctrine for these days!" This limitation, so frequently associated with the sacerdotal type, though not with it alone, is one which arises from the very nature of its ruling idea. By its proneness to lay emphasis on the authority and antiquity of the Church, and to regard the grace of God as specially mediated to man once for all by a supernatural revelation, thereafter to be transmitted only through a sacerdotal ministry and divinely appointed sacraments, it is naturally very slow to acknowledge in non-ecclesiastical forms the presence of that Spirit that bloweth where it listeth and giveth to every man severally as it will. It is a type, for instance, which may encourage the trouncing of Richard Baxter by Judge Jeffreys, or the imprisonment of John Bunyan by Justice Keelin, or the scolding of John Wesley by Bishop Butler,[1] and which may without difficulty come perilously near to blasphemy against the Holy Ghost. How often have men been anxious to preserve the channels intact which bring our streams of grace o'er hill and dale from its original, far-off fountain in the historic past, while they ignore those bubbling springs of the Spirit which have their perennial source in the human heart! And this diligence to trim the smoking wick in the horn lantern of the Church, how often has it forgotten or been blind to the rising dawn of that light which lighteth every man coming into the world!

Ruskin has reminded us, in a fine passage, that the true house of God need not be any ecclesiastical building, " but this *place*; this windy slope of Wharnside; this moorland hollow, torrent-bitten,

---

[1] " Sir, the pretending to extraordinary revelations and gifts of the Holy Ghost is a horrid thing, a very horrid thing." (Wesley, *Works*, vol. xiii. p. 465.)

snow-blighted! this *any* place where God lets down
the ladder. . . . Not that the Church is not sacred,
but that the whole earth is. I would have you
feel what careless, what constant, what infectious sin
there is in all modes of thought, whereby in calling
your churches only 'holy,' you call your hearths and
homes 'profane.'"[1] In proportion as a type of
piety exalts the Church, magnifies the power and
prerogative of the priesthood, elevates the mystery
and supernaturalism of the sacraments, and pro-
mulgates the infallibility of revealed dogma, to that
extent it is in danger of disparaging the normal
sanctities of human life, as they persist in the
common pieties and aspirations of mankind, and of
forgetting that

> "The primal duties shine aloft—like stars ;
> The charities that soothe, and heal, and bless,
> Are scattered at the feet of Man—like flowers."[2]

There is no better example of this than the
Tractarian Movement itself. Keble, Newman, and
Pusey were among the saints of the earth, men of
whom the world was not worthy, and who would
have adorned the Church of Christ in any age.

---

[1] Ruskin, *The Crown of Wild Olive*, §§ 62, 64. Compare
Sesame and Lilies, § 37. "There is a true Church wherever one
hand meets another hand helpfully, and that is the only holy or
Mother Church which ever was or ever shall be."

[2] Wordsworth, *Excursion*, ix. 238.

secration, and scant respect comes to be paid to the heart of faith which makes all places and times holy by its own transmuting power. A spiritual efficacy is even attached to the performance of ceremonies which require no religious faith either in him who performs them or in him in whose interests they are performed, and a primacy and fixity are given to elements in religion which should properly be fluid and quite secondary. When this point is reached, the formal perfection of a system may become its chief spiritual defect. It is a small matter that a Church should be organically connected with the first ages of Christianity by an unbroken line of historical continuity, if it has moved away from the spirit of Jesus and is no longer a faithful interpreter of His gospel. The worship, indeed, is made ornate and impressive, but religion suffers, inasmuch as a justification by sacraments and works has been deftly substituted for justification by faith, within the very heart of Christianity itself. The moral and religious ends for which Christ came into the world are thus no longer realized, or even aimed at. The trappings and accessories of spiritual truth are treated as identical with its essential nature. The result is that every friendly criticism of the former is treated and persecuted as a hostile assault upon the latter, and they at last who must save religion are forced into becoming the enemies of the Church.

A second defect associated with the sacerdotal type of piety is that it ever tends, in its grosser forms, to weaken and enslave the human spirit. Ideally, it should be the function of the Christian society to brace, liberalize, and develop the private conscience, purge it of its provincialisms and petty prejudices. And where this influence is freely and sympathetically exercised it is, on the whole, beneficial. The evil begins when the judgment resident in the whole society is entrusted to, or is assumed by, an official, and acquires coercive power. Then that which should emancipate becomes a tyranny. Generally speaking, the conscience which is dominated by a priest or an institution becomes enfeebled. Its spring, resilience, and spontaneity are taken out of it. It is made answerable to an earthly tribunal instead of being brought naked to the judgment seat of the King of kings.[1] The corporate conscience of the priesthood, or of the Church, is made to overrule the private conscience of the individual, and may be, often is, the poorer of the two. The priest may truly be said to thrive on a weak conscience and to make it weaker. He has persecuted and slain the prophet from the

[1] Note G.

beginning of human history. It is his aim to
monopolize the grace of God and to stereotype it
into institutions, anathematizing all who will not
conform to these, and keeping those who will in a
state of pupilage. He suspects the free movements
of the Spirit which will not take his direction or
subject themselves to his control. He exercises a
prying and harmful surveillance over the individual
conscience, especially where he can wield the
instrument of the confessional. He weakens the
sturdy moral sense of personal and inalienable
accountability for sin, and trifles with guilt by
promising it an easier relief than either God, or the
gospel, or the enlightened conscience will allow.[1]
He demands, in short, that the conscience shall
conform to ecclesiastical rather than to purely
religious standards, and warps it to the approving
of ecclesiastical pretensions, and the justifying of
ecclesiastical policy and acts. It is by no mere
accident that the sacerdotal type of piety has pro-
duced Jesuitry in religion and Machiavelism in
politics, whereas the more ethical, if sometimes
harsh and narrow, protest of the spirit of humanity

---

[1] "The Romish was a comfortable faith; Lambourne spoke
true in that. A man had but to follow his thrift by such ways as
offered—tell his beads—hear a mass—confess and be absolved.
These puritans tread a harder and a rougher path." (Scott's
Kenilworth, chap. vii.)

against corruption, tyranny, and wrong has come to be identified with the "Nonconformist conscience."

In the third place, the long association of the sacerdotal type of piety with political authority and privilege in this country has had effects which have been not wholly beneficial to our national life. The Elizabethan and Jacobean bishops no doubt thought it a matter for congratulation that Church and State in their time should be united in so close an embrace. But a price had to be paid for this alliance on which they little reckoned. For it meant that when the royal throne rocked to its foundations, as it presently did, the episcopal throne was shaken also. King Charles and his favourite Laud must both of them go to the block. The effect of these things was to make the Church of England essentially monarchical in its sympathies, to rank it definitely, in our great national conflict, on the side of tyranny,[1] and to leave the conserving of our civil and religious liberties to men who drew their piety from other springs. The type of religion fostered by Hooker and Laud and Andrewes could make staunch Royalists and Jacobites and Nonjurors in

---

[1] "Unhappily Elizabeth was succeeded by the house of Stuart, who were one and all of them weak despots. The consequence was that dissent identified itself with the national protest against misgovernment." (C. Bigg, *Wayside Sketches in Ecclesiastical History*, p. 197.)

later days, men who would fight to the death for
the rights and privileges of the Church. But it
could not produce men of the stamp of Hampden
or Oliver Cromwell, who stood forth in England's
crisis for the ideals of a free state and a free religion.
These characteristics have clung to Anglican piety
ever since. It has almost invariably been on the
side of conservatism, and privilege, and established
usage, and has never quite heartily sympathized
with democratic progress or popular aspirations and
ideals.[1] Dissent it has cordially hated as cheap and
vulgar. There have been, of course, innumerable
exceptions, and a remarkable alliance has sprung
up of late years between the sacerdotal party in the
Church of England and the forces of progressive
liberalism and democracy. Yet on the whole the
sacerdotal type of piety suits best an imperious and
aristocratic temper, and is eminently calculated to
foster the pet prejudices, traditions, and even in-
solences of the "governing classes." Its jealous
insistence on authority and submission, its slight

[1] " The Anglican is not in ordinary a persecuting Church ; it is
not inquisitorial or even inquisitive ; is perfectly well-bred, and
can shut its eyes on all proper occasions. If you let it alone, it
will let you alone. But its instinct is hostile to all change in
politics, literature, or social arts. The Church has not been the
founder of the London University, or the Mechanics' Institute, or
the Free School, or whatever aims at the diffusion of knowledge."
(Emerson, *English Traits*, chap. xiii.)

respect for either the rights or the judgments of the individual conscience, its injunction that those who would be good churchmen must " order themselves lowly and reverently to all their betters,"—these influences drift insensibly in one direction. They have been, and they are, in town and country, the accompaniments of aristocratic pretension, of political usurpation, of sacerdotal arrogance, and of social snobbery.

An even greater danger to which this type of piety is exposed is that of pettiness and externality, the reliance on the power of mere observances to save the soul. Outward forms and ordinances may be great aids to devotion, and perhaps the evangelical type of piety goes too far in seeking to dispense with them. But it is possible to go equally astray in the opposite direction, to kill all freedom and spontaneity of devotion in a round of ordinances, and to weaken the sense of personal moral responsibility by emphasizing the efficacy of rites, ceremonies, penances, and deprivations. Let but the idea be entertained that a saving virtue resides in the observances themselves, and a wide door is at once opened to all kinds of extravagance and superstition. If ceremonies have an intrinsic value, that value becomes increased with their repetition, the act rather than the motive inspiring it is held to be a thing of worth, and there is no limit to the minutiæ to which a meticulous piety will resort, in pursuing the elusive phantom of a ceremonial righteousness. The cutting off of the right hand is there, and the plucking out of the right eye, but alas! without the accompanying gain of entrance into life. The scrupulous and anxious soul busies itself in a round of ceremonies, penances, mortifications, and elaborate externalities, hoping thus to commend itself to the notice of the Eternal Father. For the glad welcome and the close embrace of the penitent, forgiven, and reconciled son there is substituted the irksome and hard service of the slave in bondage. Religion has been commercialized and made external. It is vain to attempt to argue with persons who are held in the vice of this devotional legalism, or to convince them of its entire divergence from the religion of the New Testament. Perhaps the best corrective is a little wholesome raillery or good-natured satire, the pungent sarcasm of a Swift or the *saeva indignatio* of a Milton.[1]

It is the weakness of sacerdotal piety that it so easily degenerates into formalism and externality and provides weights rather than wings to the devout spirit. A carefulness of abounding toils and minute observances leads to a religion of joylessness and

[1] Note H.

fatigue. There is much washing of cups and platters, a tithing of mint and cummin, while judgment, mercy, and faith are left neglected, and the soul trembles, with a fearful looking for judgment, lest some one jot or tittle of ceremonial requirements should be omitted. Thus Laud complains bitterly in his diary of " the waspishness of these times," or busies himself in giving minute directions for Prince Charles's private chapel in Spain to be decked with " altar, fonts, palls, linen coverings, demy carpet, four surplices, candlesticks, tapers, chalices, patens, a fine towel for the prince, other towels for the household," etc., while he is bending all energies to resist such men as Pym, Hampden, and Eliot, the trustees of the liberties of England. Pusey writes distractedly to Keble to inquire whether it would do him most good to wear haircloth next to his skin of " some sharper sort," or to lie on a hard bed and smite his breast, or to pray with his arms in the form of a cross.[1] R. Hurrell Froude records humiliatingly in his diary that he has so little succeeded in making the flesh subservient to the spirit, that he " looked with greediness to see if there was goose on the table for dinner," and even, after long fasting, indulged in buttered toast.[2] When it

[1] H. P. Liddon, *Life of E. B. Pusey*, vol. iii. p. 100.
[2] *Remains*, vol. i. pp. 15, 24.

5

comes to this it is only charitable to suppose that piety is becoming a disease and should be treated pathologically, and that the shades of the prison-house are already beginning to close over the devout soul.

We conclude, then, that the sacerdotal type of piety can show some of the saintliest names that have adorned the Church of Christ in any age. Yet it is open to lurking weaknesses and defects, which retard rather than assist a spiritual faith, and may even prove the foe to true religion. Where the sensibilities of the soul are properly attuned, it may produce characters of indescribable fragrance and charm, yet its tendency is to appeal rather to the spiritual imagination than to the redeemed conscience, and wondrously to enrich the æsthetical emotions without correspondingly strengthening the moral will. It is peculiarly exposed to those dangers which beset the sacerdotal type of faith in all countries and at all times, the danger so vividly portrayed and so sternly denounced by the ancient prophet, of trampling temple courts, and holding appointed feasts and solemn meetings, which are a weariness to Him who desires above all things a broken and a contrite spirit, with mercy for the fatherless and judgment for the oppressed. We look back on the history of the Church of England,

and think gratefully of the many glories which it has purchased for our country. We treasure the *Prayer Book*, the *Temple*, the *Preces Privatae*, and the *Christian Year*, we cherish its ancient shrines, and love those country parsonages, where holiness has been brought to a fine art, in Winchester, Bemerton, Hursley, Golden Grove, and many more. But we ask, Was this the type of piety which won for us our civil and religious liberties in the seventeenth century? Was it this which evangelized the homeland and sent out the first missionaries to the heathen in the eighteenth century? Did it even lead the way in the awakened philanthropic reform movement of the nineteenth century? To all these questions must be given the answer, No. For these advantages we are indebted to men of another mould and of a different faith, who were reared on a type of piety we must seek elsewhere.

THE EVANGELICAL TYPE

I

THE evangelical type of piety, to which we now turn, is based on a profound conviction of the holiness of God, the sin of man, and the reconciliation of these two by free redeeming grace and justifying faith. It is unnecessary here to follow the intricacies of theological speculation on these subjects which have developed since the Reformation, or to trace the differences between Calvinism and Arminianism with respect to the decrees of God, the extent of human depravity, the scope of the Atonement, the resistibility of grace, or the perseverance of the elect. Roughly speaking, Calvinism inclined to look on these problems from the divine standpoint, Arminianism from the human. The former emphasized God's sole sovereignty, the latter our co-operating freedom. And the differences involved had far-reaching effects on the religious, political, ethical, and social development of modern Europe, Calvinism giving birth to Puritanism in the seventeenth century, and Arminianism to the Evangelical Revival a century later. The point to be remembered in the present connection, however, is this, that the cleavage which separated them did not reach down to the rock on which they both rested. In repudiating sacerdotalism and a mediating priesthood, in claiming the right of the believer to have direct access to Christ as the sole Head of the Church, and in contending for a reconciliation with God which was mediated objectively by the Atonement and subjectively by faith alone, Calvinism and Arminianism were at one, and rested upon a common basis of evangelical belief.

The first article, then, of the evangelical faith is the holiness of God. The God of evangelicalism is not that good-natured and indulgent Being whom the natural man so hopefully but weakly worships. Still less is He that non-moral, non-personal essence, the God of pantheism, a God who expresses Himself indifferently in the riotings of a Rabelais and the sighings of a Thomas à Kempis. The God of evangelicalism is the God whom Isaiah and Paul and Augustine and Luther and Calvin have made known unto us, a God high and lifted up, inhabiting eternity, who is of purer eyes than to behold iniquity, and who will by no means clear the guilty. Evangelicals are always peculiarly at home in the Old

Testament, and they are the trustees of the Hebraic consciousness in religion. Their God, even though His name be Love, is a consuming fire. He is a heavenly Sovereign, Lawgiver, and Judge, as well as Father, one whose holiness is to be feared and whose laws must be obeyed, a God whose wrath thunders ominously in the clouds of Sinai, and even whose love lightens magnificently by terrible things in righteousness from the Cross of Calvary.

Before two such burning mountains as these it is evident that the helpless mortal sinner must exceedingly fear and quake. His own righteousness shrivels up before them both, and becomes as filthy rags. While such a God is in heaven and he on earth, his words will be few. Rather, they will be none at all, for every mouth is stopped, boasting is excluded, all men are shut up under sin, utterly impotent to save themselves or extenuate their guilt, in the face of the awful contrast between their own highest perfections and God's most holy claims. This "law work" is an indispensable preliminary to the true understanding of the gospel. The whole evangelical system is grounded on the sense of sin. Its three R's, so to speak, are those of Ruin, Redemption, and Regeneration. Wherever men are not conscious of their sin, or wherever evil is conceived not religiously as guilt but philosophically as negation, or pathologically as disease, or evolutionally as imperfection, or socially as crime or as bad manners, there the evangelical doctrines of Christianity are bound to fail of their appeal. Evangelicalism, it should be noted, is not tied to the acceptance of the Genesis story of the Fall of Man, nor is it bound up with any theory of total depravity or original sin. It is enough that man as we know him, and as he has always been, invariably grieves and resists the Holy Spirit. Even if there still survive within us the once harmless and natural forces of an earlier and more savage stage of our development, the moment these survivals become anachronisms, and are cherished in opposition to divine forces that make for righteousness and moral progress, sin enters, and the historico-traditional allegory of the Fall becomes a psychological and spiritual fact of our experience. Evil, in evangelicalism, need not have its root in any spiritual Power or powers alien to ourselves, tempting and soliciting us to sin. Nor is it necessary that any of the materials presented to us in experience should be evil in themselves. The mischief may lie solely in the evil will, which fails to moralize wholly these given elements, and so brings on a spiritual condition of disease. In any case, if there be no such disease, the need for a gospel to remove it must disappear.

"They that are whole have no need of a physician, but they that are sick." Evangelicalism either finds men in this sick condition or it puts them into it, as its first business. It seeks to "convince men of sin, judgment, and righteousness to come," and has no patience with any kind of reliance on self-righteousness, ceremonies, or good works, as commending us to God. Its aim is to provoke men to the spirit of bondage whereby they fear, ere it will admit them to the joys of the spirit of adoption whereby they cry, Abba, Father.

When a man has been thus crushed and humbled with the sense of guilt, his first concern will naturally be with the problem of how he is to be freed from his wretched and forlorn condition. He is at the foot of a well, as it were, sunk in some fearful pit and miry clay, and paralyzed to boot. His one urgent business is to find some means of being delivered from his misery. He is in no mood for art, literature, or the pleasures of this world, even supposing them to be within reach. His case is too desperate for these emollients, and he cannot bide their trifling. With God's righteous judgments hanging over him, his eternal weal or woe suspended in the balance so that a single hair may turn the scale between life and death, what can he do but shut his ears to every other consideration, and cry

out as Christian did in *The Pilgrim's Progress*,
"Eternal Life! Eternal Life! What must I do
to be saved and win Eternal Life?"

The answer is that he is to be saved not so much
by doing as by believing. He must rely on what
God can do in him, and has already done for him,
and yet will do through him, by Christ Jesus.
When a man is in a pit, lame from his mother's
womb, by neither repentance, nor sacrifices, nor
tears, nor prayers, nor worldly wisdom, nor good
works, can he lift himself out. He can only *be* lifted
out, and it is the glory of evangelicalism that it
affirms this to be actually done for us by God in
Christ, who not only descends the pit and raises us
out of it, but who heals our constitutional lameness
as well, sets our feet upon a rock and puts a new
song into our mouth, even praise unto our God.

All this is accomplished by the energies of grace,
and it is important to remember that the word
'grace,' in the evangelical conception of Christianity,
has a different connotation from that which it bears
in the sacerdotal. Its affinities are free, personal,
prophetic, ethical, and spiritual, rather than close,
priestly, episcopal, institutional, and ecclesiastical.
It is not a kind of divine substance or virtue infused
into humanity to assist our frailty, and transmitted
by valid sacraments through properly appointed

channels, to purge our grosser nature with its purifying flame. It is rather a personal attitude and moral relationship between two living and independent wills, the act of a holy and loving Father towards His erring children, in so dealing with them as to condemn and chastise their sin, and forgive it, and turn it into holiness. When man was in so woeful a plight that nothing he could do of himself could put him right, and when there was no eye to pity and no arm to save, God's own eye pitied and His own arm brought salvation in a great act of deliverance.

The doctrine of the Atonement is thus a cardinal article of the evangelical creed. It was a remedy demanded by the critical moral situation of the sinfulness of man and the holiness of God. In such a pass the will of God moved Him to redeem, the wisdom of God contrived the way, and the love of God shrank not from the cost. In the supreme emergency of human history the grace of God was equal to all demands. A cosmic victory was won and a full atonement wrought by the humiliation of the eternal Son, who was made man in the manger of Bethlehem and made sin on the Cross of Calvary ; who through the eternal Spirit offered unto God that perfect sacrifice of an active and complete holiness which we had failed to render, conquered

to that strong arm so graciously stretched down to raise us up. Like the words 'sin' and 'grace,' which we have already been considering, the word 'faith,' in the evangelical conception, has a signification of its own which should be clearly grasped. The sacerdotal conception of faith is that it is an acceptance of truth upon authority apart from its content, an attitude of obedient receptivity towards those influences of grace which stream down upon us from the supersensible world, in the Incarnation first of all, and then in the prescribed channels of ecclesiastical institutions. The evangelical conception is more ethical. It is the turning of the whole man to an object inherently worthy, the reception and the appropriation of the living Christ Himself by the direct, priestless, individual response of the free soul to His free, redeeming, and justifying grace, and its consequent complete identification with Him in His saving energies and purposes for mankind. Justification by faith thus comes to mean the acceptance of the totality of the soul's goodwill, on the part of God and for Christ's sake, in lieu of its ever-defective single works of righteousness. Evangelicalism attaches little importance to the officially mediating Church in the work of salvation, but lays the greatest stress on the immediate action of God on the soul, and on the uninterrupted access of the soul to God, in which all intermediaries but Christ are brushed aside. In short, it relies implicitly on the words of the New Testament, "Believe on the Lord Jesus Christ and thou shalt be saved."

The attraction of this type of piety will be immediately manifest. Its strength lies in its simplicity, its directness, its spiritual grandeur, and in the instant and complete reconciliation which it so freely offers to faith alone. Weary, sick, helpless, conscious of his sin, and despairing of ever attaining to righteousness of life, the sinner is not asked to go through some purifying penances in the hope of thus commending himself to the righteousness of God, but is received at once to the Father's embrace, just as he is, without one plea save that the arms of the Cross have been stretched out to welcome him. In adoring wonder at such unmerited and overflowing love the heart melts, the will breaks down, the conscience is absolved, and the whole being of the sinner is gratefully surrendered to the Saviour of the world. And lo, in the very act, he is born or regenerated from above. A new life pulses within him as from the indwelling Christ. By the supreme leap of faith and the act of God's new creation, joined in one, he is transferred from the realm of nature to the realm of grace, and from having been a servant he becomes a son. Being a new creature, all things about him become new in consequence. Earth becomes vocal, and duty sweet, and the clouds which obscured the heavens have passed away. He knows himself justified by faith and accepted in the Beloved, not by works of righteousness which he has done or yet may do, but because of his trust in the mercy and love of God his Saviour. The burden of his guilt falls loosened from his back, and is lost within the sepulchre at the foot of his Master's Cross, so that with light and bounding steps he goes upon his way. The consequences of his sin remain, it is true, but they are changed from the punishments of wrath to the chastisements of love. The innumerable vicissitudes and trials to be endured but work out his salvation and bring him nearer God, and he knows that the same grace which so miraculously saved him, and delivered him from his sin, is able to keep him from falling back again into the mire from which he has escaped, and will, after he has suffered a little while, perfect, stablish, strengthen him, and at last present him faultless before the presence of God's glory with exceeding joy.[1]

It is inevitable that experiences such as these will very profoundly affect a man's conception of the

[1] Note I.

Church. Having been made a member of Christ without the mediation of a priesthood, what more natural than that he should continue to dispense with it? If Christians are united to their Lord by a living faith, are they not free to model the institutions of the Church according to the requirements of His indwelling Spirit?[1] Nay, are they not bound to make the Church the faithful social expression of that gospel by which they have been individually redeemed, the community, namely, of those who, by a like exercise of faith, have come into a like personal relation to the grace of the redeeming Lord? Evangelicalism, as a formative principle, is indifferent to questions of Church polity, and has been historically the parent of many denominations of Christians, for it is tolerant of diversities of organization as well as of creed, so long as its central principle is conserved. It is rather a force issuing in Churches than a Church force. Whereas sacerdotalism clings to valid orders, and the purity and uniformity of a divinely appointed organization, as necessary to the very being of the

---

[1] " In the Christian society, the General Will seeking the good of each in the good of the whole, and expressing the deeper self of the society, is, so the Church believes, none other than the voice of the Holy Spirit. And the supreme purpose of all Church organization should be to give to this voice an adequate vehicle for the utterance of itself." (J. H. B. Masterman, *Rights and Responsibilities of National Churches*, p. 35.)

Church, evangelicalism concerns itself rather with a unity of the Spirit underlying wide divergencies of form. It believes that the sacerdotal limiting of the full stream of divine grace to certain prescribed channels is a denial of its very essence, and that the real presence of Christ is confined neither to one Sacrament, nor to one Church, nor to all the Churches. The function of the Church is to make Christians. It is to engender penitence, and faith, and love, and to advance in every land the kingdom of our God. That form of organization, therefore, is necessarily the best which in any given circumstances the Spirit chooses, and which is found best to promote the purposes of the gospel.

Not all who call themselves evangelicals, of course, would subscribe to these conclusions, for evangelicalism, as a principle of faith, is much wider than Nonconformity. Yet it is hardly possible to speak of evangelicalism, on the side of organization, without dealing chiefly with that Nonconformity into which it characteristically and inevitably develops.[1] The theory of gathered as distinct from national Churches is implicit in the very nature of evangelical faith. It is bound up with it logically and flows from it historically. The Church Invisible is made up of all those who savingly believe in the Lord

[1] Note J.

Jesus Christ, who love Him in sincerity and in truth. Should not the Church Visible, so far as possible, be the same? Should not the wheat be gathered into barns? And where two or three are gathered together in the divine name, must not Christ be present, and with Christ the Church? There is no doubt a grave difficulty in knowing who are to be styled Christians on such a basis, especially if the determining voice be left with those who are most ready to profess loudly that they are such. In that case the elect would be few indeed, and reapers would rush in where even the garnering angels wait until the harvest. But is it not at least likely that a prayerfully constituted company of sincere believers will correspond more nearly to the visible Body of our Lord than a miscellaneous company of all who have been ceremoniously baptized, and who were " made members of Christ, the children of God, and inheritors of the kingdom of heaven " in infancy?

To consistent evangelicalism the true *ecclesia* or Church is the general assembly of the enfranchised, who are "sanctified in Christ Jesus, called to be saints, with all that call upon the name of our Lord Jesus Christ in every place, their Lord and ours."[1] It is a society in which all are priests, by the

[1] 1 Cor. i. 2.

spiritual indwelling of the one High Priest in every member, and which is held together by no official hierarchy or fixed organization, but by the life which pulses through each limb from the one Head. It is the advance guard of humanity, the company of the redeemed whom no man can number, Christ in His social aspect, the society of the Holy Ghost, the moving area of the Cross, God's pillar of cloud and fire marking out the path of human progress and destiny. In New Testament phraseology the Church is a spiritual house, a holy priesthood, an elect race, a people for God's own possession, consisting of those who have been called out of darkness into His marvellous light. It is a community which will be a theocracy, inasmuch as it is subject to the sole authority of God in Christ. It will also be a democracy, since its members share an equal and universal priesthood, and a community of spiritual responsibilities, privileges, and rights, however they may distribute formal offices and functions. But chiefly will it be an aristocracy, inasmuch as those who compose it have, by their oneness with Christ, been made separate from the world.

The sacerdotal and evangelical types, then, differ widely and essentially both in ultimate principle and in historical development. The former maintains the thesis that, properly speaking, Christ is coterminous with His Church. The latter essays the task of moulding a Church or Churches that shall be coterminous with Christ. *Both* take up the standpoint that the Church is the home of Christ's grace, the normal channel of His Spirit, the means by which His love is to be mediated to the world. *Both* would equally contend that men cannot properly coalesce into a church by voluntary agreement and association, but that there is one true Church of Christ in heaven and on earth into which they have to be invited. From this point, however, the attitudes diverge, especially where the types are developed to extremes. The Romanist then approaches the individual from the standpoint of the Church, and would have men join the Church that so they may become Christians, by virtue of that grace which it, and it alone, is commissioned to dispense. The Nonconformist approaches the Church, on the other hand, from the standpoint of the individual, and would have those only to constitute the Church who are already Christians by virtue of that grace which is theirs through faith in Christ. The one is strict to test apostolicity by succession. The other will test succession itself by apostolicity. He claims that the gospel makes the Church and not the Church the gospel, and that the

Spirit accompanies the gospel rather than ecclesiastically valid sacraments.

The evangelical party in the Church of England occupy a somewhat peculiar and anomalous position in this respect. No one can question the rich contribution which they have made to our national religious life. Romaine, Venn, Grimshawe, Fletcher, Newton, Cowper, Scott, and Simeon, to mention only the later examples, are great names, and they claim their rightful place in a Church which is as evangelical in its articles as it is sacerdotal in its liturgy. Many of the High Church clergy, too, are earnestly evangelical, in the wider sense of the word, and it may be said that the sacraments themselves are steeped in evangelical teaching. Yet the true evangelical principle has never found itself, so to speak, within the borders of the Church of England. It has been compelled, both in the Nonconformist ejections of the seventeenth century and in the Wesleyan revival of the eighteenth, to seek its freest and fullest expression somewhere else. Evangelical clergymen may have cordially fraternized with their Free Church brethren on the Exeter Hall platform or in the tents at Keswick. But the standards of their own Church stubbornly prevent an equal and reciprocal communion. They must be institutional first of all, and evangelical afterwards. In nothing is the compromising position of the Anglican Church as a *via media* more apparent. It carries out neither of its contending principles to a final issue, but leaves the logical development of its sacerdotal principle to Roman Catholicism, and of its evangelical principle to Nonconformity.

The evangelical Nonconformist does not feel, however, that in dispensing with the priests and sacraments of a sacerdotal Church he is sacrificing anything essential. Rites and ceremonies *may* be aids to faith; they may also be the reverse. In themselves they are indifferent, for it is not in them but in the faith that the efficacy resides. Priesthood and Holy Baptism may assist much, but, like circumcision, they are of no avail without the new creature; and the sacraments, equally with the sabbath, were made for man, not man for the sacraments. The Nonconformist is therefore well content to do without imposing adjuncts to his religion, being satisfied with the sheer majesty and truth of the gospel's own appeal. As for the alleged bareness of his worship, he feels that it is more seemly to approach God in a homely dress than in a gaudy one, and that his soul has something more urgent and appealing to say to God than the language of artifice and convention can express.[1]

[1] " I had heard the service of high mass in France, celebrated with

Being a son of the Father, he will speak as the Spirit moves him, not as state or bishop may direct, for he is assured that his spontaneous exclamations of love and praise, however stammering, will be more acceptable to the Father than the most chastely ordered ritual that remains cold and formal. Nor does he feel that he is missing anything in not surrounding his worship with the mystery of chiselled stone and painted glass. Enough if, within bare walls and out upon the lone and windy moor, he can soar into those chambers of celestial imagery, all tapestried with the counsels of the Eternal Father, which sufficed for the writer of *Grace Abounding* on Elstow Green, or the author of *Paradise Lost* in Bunhill Fields.

To the evangelical the one complete outfit and indispensable *vade mecum* is the Bible. That is his guide, philosopher, and friend, the plain man's pathway to heaven, his armoury for the fight, his storehouse and treasury of things new and old, in which are contained all things necessary to salvation. Whereas the sacerdotalist brings a great variety of

all the éclat which the choicest music, the richest dresses, the most imposing ceremony, could confer upon it ; yet it fell short in effect of the simplicity of the Presbyterian worship. The devotion, in which every one took a share seemed so superior to that which was recited by musicians, as a lesson which they had learned by rote, that it gave the Scottish worship all the advantage of reality over acting." (Scott, *Rob Roy*, chap. xx.)

devotional manuals with him into the secret place, and tends to become much more at home in his prayer-book and breviary than in the Word of God, the typical evangelical is content to feed his piety on the Bible and on little else. There may be both advantages and disadvantages in this position. *Grace Abounding* and *The Pilgrim's Progress* show what a sinewy and graphic style, as well as what richness of spiritual experience, may result from a close study of the Book of books; yet there can be little doubt that John Bunyan himself, like many another good evangelical, would have been much happier in his mind, as well as a great deal more enlightened in his opinions, could he have had a larger library and compared, as a good churchman would have done, the teaching of the Bible with that of reason, authority, and the traditions of the Church. Hardness and literalism of interpretation, a mechanical and superstitious reverence for every syllable, a disposition to look upon the Word as a kind of infallible oracle upon every subject,[1] and to find by the aid of cross-references and mystical allusions all kinds of hidden,

---

[1] Thus Berridge, the evangelical rector of Everton, was prevented from marrying because, on consulting his Bible as to whether or no he should "take a Jezebel," as he termed it, his eye lighted on a text that was unfavourable to matrimony. See Lecky's *History of England*, vol. ii. p. 622.

allegorical meanings where none are intended, these are some of the disadvantages attendant on a too exclusive elevation of the Bible as a source of authority in religion. Yet how compensating are the advantages! Granted that the exegesis of the man who, like Bunyan, is "seldom out of the Bible," may be in some instances sadly wide of the mark, he has nevertheless a clue to its general significance which will never permit him to wander far astray. The true interpreter of the Bible is neither the Higher Criticism nor an authoritative Church, but the evangelical experience of an awakened heart.

The evangelical's *final* seat of authority, that is to say, is not the letter but the spirit, not the Bible itself but the gospel within the Bible. Just as evangelicalism, as a principle, is patient of many differences both in theological opinion and in Church polity, so also is it historically compatible with widely divergent views on the authority of scripture. Sometimes the greatest freedom has been brought to the interpretation of the Bible, and its different parts have been regarded as wheat or straw according as the doctrines of grace have been emphasized or overlooked. Sometimes the whole has been regarded as equally inspired, and erected into an infallible authority as compact and invulnerable as

the Catholic Church itself. Sometimes only matters
of faith have been deduced from its pages, as these
may be determined by private judgment and the
governing control of the Holy Spirit. Sometimes
the sacred oracle has been indifferently searched in
Judges and *Revelation* for principles of domestic
economy, ecclesiastical government, or civil business.
Calvinism has appealed to the Bible as supporting
one set of doctrines, Arminianism another. The
allegorist has claimed that foregleams of the gospel
shine forth from wayside verses in *Ezekiel* or
Leviticus. The modern critic has sought to prune
down these luxurious fancies and to confine us to
the exact and literal meaning of the first authors
and nothing more. Yet all these may be, and
indeed have been, evangelicals, and they serve to
establish the principle, a principle not always
explicit, but really implicit in this type of piety
from the first, that the final authority in evangelicalism is the evangel. Whereas the Romanist
relies ultimately on the utterances of the Pope, and
the Anglican sacerdotalist maintains the principle,
"The Church to teach, the Bible to confirm," and
the Quaker turns from all outward authority to the
inner voice, the Evangelical finds his determining
authority in none of these, but in God's redeeming
act in the person, life, and death of the Lord Christ,

makes heavy demands on the soul, rules out a facile sacramentalism, and favours the production of men of a strong and intense type, who faithfully face the facts of sin's paralysis, and the need of some divine deliverance and renewal if holiness is to be achieved. It will thus tend to attract to itself the more passionate, impulsive, and even tempestuous natures, psychologically, the twice-born, as they have been called, men who enter into life after some sharp severe crisis of inward struggle. They will be men living under an awed sense of the glory of their redemption, and the price at which it has been purchased for them; narrow, perhaps, and sturdily bigoted and intolerant, yet strong, masculine, and self-reliant, carrying an air of high moral dignity and grave seriousness, as of men who have attained, through conflict, to peace in believing, and who know themselves to be elect, with their names written in heaven, the very tools and instruments of the Eternal Will. As such they will be men prompt in resolution and firm in action, ready to launch fearlessly and joyously upon the high enterprise of remodelling a world, relying on things inner rather than things outer, sure of themselves because sure of the mission with which they have been entrusted of wresting a kingdom of light from the surrounding darkness, and knowing

modern state. Toleration and voluntaryism in religion, the emphasis on experience in theology, liberty, self-government, and enfranchisement in politics, the resistance to the Stuart tyranny, the rise of the capitalistic system, and the development of our commercial and industrial prosperity as a nation, all have their spiritual roots in Puritan evangelicalism.[1]

Of course it would be claiming too much to contend that evangelicalism either created or has ever had a monopoly of those virtues of sturdy independence and self-reliance which are among our most distinctive racial attributes. But it may certainly be said that it has immensely strengthened them. If the sacerdotal type of piety ministers to our national conservatism and restraint and love of order, the evangelical nurtures our more radical energies of enterprise and daring and reform and independence. " The secret of the Empire is in the men whom Britain sends forth in their freedom, courage, mastery, and wisdom, in the resource and the responsibility developed by their having to act alone, without instructions, and without immediate supervision. It is not the English Parliament nor

---

[1] See two interesting articles by P. T. Forsyth, D.D., on "Calvinism and Capitalism," in *The Contemporary Review*, June and July, 1910.

the English Constitution that is felt in the English proconsul on the skirts of the Himalayas, but the English *man*. . . . But what does that mean? It means that our power is in its nature and genius Protestant and not Catholic, that its salvation is the development of individual resource and responsibility; that its doom would be to settle down into mere officialism, to set up the priestly idea of responsibility for the Protestant, and to regard the ideal Englishman more as a machine to obey orders than as a living moral centre of freedom, confidence, and power. Make your religion Catholic, and above all things institutional, and in due time you reduce English enterprise to something in the nature of a Jesuit mission, the Englishman abroad to a political cleric, the merchant to a retailer, and the great firm to the spirit of a tied house. . . . It would be an article of faith to bow to the priest as a part of the soul's homage to God, to think of the priest as a minor god. And to the soul's faith both in itself and in God that is fatal, and it has been shown by the atheism of Catholic Europe so to be." [1]

There are two ways in which the evangelical spirit ever seeks to express itself in the wider life of the world, one of which is political and the other missionary. Its activities, indeed, in the former

[1] P. T. Forsyth, *Rome, Reform and Reaction*, pp. 168, 169.

direction, are viewed with disfavour in some quarters. It is stated, for example, that certain evangelical Churches of to-day are rearing politicians rather than saints, and that their buildings are the committee rooms and lecture halls of a political party rather than places set apart for the worship of God. But these charges arise from a misapprehension of the true genius of evangelical faith. The type of saint developed by an evangelical Church is usually different from that canonized by a sacerdotal Church, and it is not to be expected that the one will fully understand the other. Catholicism does not produce saints in the Protestant sense, nor does Protestantism produce saints in the Catholic sense, although these may be complementary the one to the other. Thus Catholicism approaches God through the sensuous imagination and spiritual affections, and aims at ecstasy, transport, fruition, an ascetic sanctity and aloofness from the world, a holiness which aspires to attain, through Purgatory, to the awful and unutterable bliss of the Beatific Vision, and would fain burn in the Sacred Heart, or be pierced with the seven wounds of the Blessed Jesus. Protestantism takes a more ethical direction, and seeks to approach God through the redeemed conscience, the moral will, and the establishment of a righteous state.[1]

[1] The issue, as seen from the Catholic point of view, may be

realization of His moral ends in the customs and constitution of society.[1] It is inevitable that these two ideals of holiness will produce two altogether different types of Christian saint. The one will give birth to the priest and the ascetic, the other to the prophet and the reformer. The one will withdraw saintliness to the cloister, and cherish a clerical and retired holiness. The other will cultivate saintliness in homes, in senates, and in market-places, and produce some of its most shining examples of holiness from among the laity.

It is probably true that the Puritans, in these matters, occupied an extreme position. They coerced where they should have wooed. They attempted to force the pace too quickly in matters of national righteousness, and looked with too unfriendly an eye on mince-pies, maypoles, and madrigals, as having no clear tendency to bring in the kingdom of God. But at least they were animated by a great and

---

[1] " We that serve you beg of you not to own us, but God alone. We pray you own His people more and more ; for they are the chariots and horsemen of Israel. Disown yourselves, but own your Authority ; and improve it to curb the proud and the insolent, such as would disturb the tranquillity of England. Relieve the oppressed, hear the groans of poor prisoners. Be pleased to reform the abuses of all professions, and if there be any one that makes many poor to make a few rich, that suits not a Commonwealth." (Oliver Cromwell, *Letter to Speaker Lenthall*, after the Battle of Dunbar, 1650.)

7

noble faith. They believed in a divine order such
as should rule all the political, social, and domestic
concerns of human life. They believed that God
had made known that divine order, in Milton's proud
phrase, "as His manner is, first to Englishmen."
And they believed that human law and order should
be rudely shattered, if need be, to make way for the
divine.[1] And if sometimes they grasped too readily
at carnal weapons for the attainment of spiritual
ends, it was because they looked for new heavens
and a new earth in which dwelleth righteousness,
and dreamed of a happy and sober England in
which the profligacies of Whitehall and the de-
baucheries of the village alehouse should be alike
unknown.

Finally, the evangelical spirit freely and necessarily issues in evangelism. Missions ever follow in
the wake of the true reception of the gospel. He
who has once had a genuine experience of divine
grace, who can look backward with a kind of
shuddering horror to the yawning pit of sin from
which he has been delivered, and forward to the
goal for the prize of his high calling in Christ Jesus,

[1] "They say the government of episcopacy is now weaved into
the common law. In God's name let it weave out again; let not
human quillets keep back divine authority. It is not the common
law, nor the civil, but piety and justice that are our foundresses."
(Milton, *Reformation in England*.)

will be irresistibly constrained by the love of Christ to bring the same salvation to others also. Condemned, redeemed, justified, and made a new creature at the Cross, he realizes how tragic must be the fate of those who miss the way of life. And so, knowing the fear of the Lord, he seeks to persuade men, and is ready to go out into the highways and hedges with the message of the gospel, feeling it the first of all duties to rescue perishing sinners from their dangerous condition. For what conceivable reason has he been mercifully turned from darkness to light and from the power of Satan unto God, unless it be in order that he may straightway go forth, a missionary to the gentiles, to open blind eyes and extend the kingdom of God. This passion for souls, this divine yearning of pity for the last, the least, and the lost, this burning desire that *all* men may be saved and brought to the knowledge of the truth, is the most essential, as it is the most attractive, characteristic of the evangelical type of piety. It is not the first concern of the evangelist to divide men up into grades and classes, as the institutional Church does, and to pray for kings, soldiers, etc., as they may *severally* need. What he is anxious to press upon all alike is the one supremely urgent appeal, that they should flee from the wrath to come and believe in the Lord

The reform of prisons, however, and the emancipation of slaves are properly to be regarded as but the by-products of evangelicalism, the subsidiary social results of its spiritual triumphs. For it is a strange yet true fact, that the type of piety which is most egoistic in its creed, and lays supreme emphasis on the saving of the individual, has proved to be the type which has done most to create the social conscience, and serve the interests of collective humanity. The religion which seems above all others to be unworldly and even other-worldly in its aims has been that which abounds most in practical benevolence, and produces the greatest social, political, and philanthropic as well as moral and spiritual reforms. " If the Reformation has been a blessing to Europe," says Dr. Martineau, who is constrained to admire the good works of a type of piety with whose doctrines he has not the remotest sympathy, " if it has not only roused its understanding but shaken off many a corruption from its conscience; if its delay was marked by growth of servility and sloth, and its establishment by improved industry, sobriety, and order, by a more elevated estimate of human rights, and a more energetic sympathy with the oppressed and outcast, it must be remembered that on the very front of this great social Revolution was inscribed the very

tenet [of justification by faith] which we conceive so full of danger. And among the churches to which the Reformation has given birth, those churches which have distinguished themselves by their powerful and beneficent effects, by their determined resistance to some social crime, by their dauntless protests against the corruption of a court or the oppression of a people, will be found to have been characterized by their attachment to the same notion. . . . Heathenism and slavery abroad, ignorance and depravity in our population at home, have been grappled with most strenuously by Christians of the same class. . . . Christianity has never manifested itself in so affectionate, disinterested, and energetic a spirit as in Churches which, like the evangelical, lay great stress on the doctrine of justification by faith."[1] These are generous words to come from a convinced opponent of the whole system of evangelicalism. Yet they are true. Reforms in all directions begin to appear when a new life is generated in the soul through faith in the living God and in the redeeming Christ." "Everything shall live whither the river cometh."[2]

There seem to be periods in the history of a nation when it lapses into moral degeneracy and

[1] *National Duties*, p. 122. [2] Ezek. xlvii. 9.

spiritual decay. We have the spectacle of a slumbering sacerdotal church and an inept theological liberalism lazily lamenting the decadence of faith. When the leaders thus grow languid and begin to question whether or no there be a gospel, it is not to be wondered at if the masses of men around them sink into practical heathenism. Then there comes into their midst a man sent from God, who lifts once again the banner of the Cross. Words which had begun to lose their meaning, such as sin and grace, redemption, justification, salvation through faith in Christ, are recalled from the writings of theologians, and pass into common speech again, to wield all their old magic and exert their former spell. The stream of religious life, which has been suffered to meander sluggishly over flat marshes, finds some narrow gorge again, and once more there is life and music in its flow. Such revivals of spiritual faith, when they do come, are almost invariably attended by the evangelical note. It is a return of the Church to her first love and to her former works, the proclamation of that gospel which was given her at the beginning, the message of an eternal love of God which has atoned for human sin, and which offers free forgiveness, restoration, and eternal life, to every child that has wandered from the Father's home.

command them to be dried up, or he is clenching his teeth to keep back the awful sin against the Holy Ghost. We discover him in stables, in barns, in milk-houses, at suits with God. We are present when he overhears the conversation of four poor women in the town of Bedford, engaged in savoury talk of the sweetness of the gospel. And we even come upon him when he is lying in bed beside his weeping wife, who is travailing with child.

The temperaments of the two men were not dissimilar. Each was of imagination all compact. Andrewes had an imagination of the comprehensive universal order, and could summon to his presence saints, angels, and archangels, and all the gathered ranks of the Church, visible and invisible. These he could marshal in meet forms of worship, interpreting all their needs, and setting them in their several relationships one to another. Bunyan's imagination was of the more intense pictorial sort. He could visualize transcendent spiritual realities with extraordinary vividness, especially as they affected his own soul. To him heaven and hell were real, and the earth a shadow, and the most important personages in all the universe were Satan and Jesus Christ. The former would pull him by the clothes occasionally, telling him he had prayed enough, and that he might as well bend the knee to

were not dissimilar, in their mode of approaching God they were widely different. The former is a striking example of the ecclesiastical or Catholic type of piety, the latter of the strongly evangelical or individualistic. Andrewes, as we have seen, even in his most intense moments was never forgetful of his place in the universal order. But Bunyan was throughout oblivious to all else but the absorbing and momentous dialogue that was going on between God and his own soul. We do, indeed, here and there in his book have a glimpse of the wider world in which he lived, and the Quakers, Ranters, Perfectionists of the time occasionally cross its pages. But even these are introduced only as minor characters remotely connected with his own inner drama, a drama which swells in its proportions till it fills heaven and earth. The age in which he wrote was one in which England was reverberating from end to end with the noise of great events. Bloody armies had clashed in civil conflict. King and archbishop had fallen from their thrones. Yet no echo of these agitations visits the distracted thoughts of this village tinker, who is far more concerned as to whether he is worse by a hair than the apostate Judas, or what would happen to him should he be killed by the falling bell of Elstow steeple. Bunyan in one place expresses his surprise

that men should make such an ado about losing wife
or child. What does that matter, when compared
with the losing of the soul? We are throughout
called upon to witness the paroxysms and struggles
of a drowning man, who feels himself sinking
beneath his own blasphemies and the divine judgments, so that all God's billows go over him, and he
has no thought for anything but to cry from the
depths that a hand should be stretched out to rescue
him from his distress.

And a hand *is* stretched out, but it is not the
hand of the Church, with its rites and ceremonies
and disciplinary hygiene. With others of a like
faith, Bunyan had a prejudice against help from
that quarter, and turned from it deliberately to the
Bible, and the Bible only. Here we come upon
another fundamental difference between him and
Andrewes. The latter had learned in the school of
Hooker to associate Reason and Tradition with the
Bible as a source of authority. From his pastor,
John Gifford, Bunyan had learned "not to take
up any truth upon trust—as from this, or that, or
any other man or men—but to cry mightily to God
that He would convince us of the reality thereof,
and set us down therein, by His own Spirit, in the
Holy Word." To Andrewes, accordingly, the Bible
was as an inexhaustible quarry from which might be

fetched innumerable many-coloured chips to frame the exquisitely wrought mosaic of his devotions. To Bunyan it was nothing less awful than the scroll of doom.

What course Bunyan might have run had he had a kindly Jesuit to advise him at this point, or could he have listened to and trusted some father-confessor, such as Dr. Pusey, we do not know. All he had to guide him to the Celestial City were the Scriptures and his own conscience as illuminated by the Holy Spirit. He desired nothing more. Of all the temptations that assailed him, the worst was that Satan should use sleights to make him doubt the written word, and they had many a tug and pull together for " that blessed sixth of John." It is true he was hard put to it at times, because of his belief that the Bible was the authentic voice of God from *Genesis* to *Revelation*. The Scriptures would " look grimly" at him, or stand like a spear against him, every refractory text being like an army of 40,000 men to afflict his spirit. The fact that the Scripture cannot be broken, he tells us, would rend the very caul of his heart, and he was weighed down unto despair for days and months and years by that verse in *Hebrews* which says that Esau " found no place of repentance, though he sought it diligently with tears." This and other passages " pinched

of the sorely tried tinker of Bedford, and were great
encouragements to him.   One passage of Scripture
was particularly helpful, and that was " when Christ
prays against Judas, that God would disappoint
him in all his selfish thoughts, which moved him to
sell his master: pray read it soberly, Ps. cix. vv.
6–20." We smile at this allegorizing and literalism
of interpretation, a literalism which made Bunyan
very puzzled to know how God Himself could sur-
mount the difficulties it presents.   " I could think
thus with myself," he writes.   " Why, how many
Scriptures are against me?   There are but three or
four, and cannot God miss them and save me from
all of them?"   Yet it was just this same scriptural-
ism and absorption in one book, and in one book
only, which has given us the pungent, pithy, and
pregnant English of one of the greatest classics in
the whole religious literature of the world.

Temperament, then, and the study of the Bible,
wrought in Bunyan to produce those experiences
which are distinctively evangelical.   First of all the
Spirit convinced him mightily of his sin.   He tells
us that "he lay long at Sinai," and that "the glory
of the holiness of God did break him in pieces."
There are passages in *Grace Abounding* which are
very painful reading.   God scares and affrights this
poor sinner with fearful dreams and surrounds him

friends and from home; or like a child that has fallen into a mill pit, and makes what shift it can to " scrabble and spraul " in the water, yet can find neither handhold nor foothold and so must perish; or like a horse sinking in the mire even in the act of flouncing toward solid ground.   What was he to do? Was he too late for mercy, and had he the mark of Cain upon his brow?   Was he *fallen away* from grace, or only *fallen* from it?   Had he put Christ to *open* shame, or only shamed Him?   These differences were vital, and he was tortured to find an answer. If he prayed after rejecting the mediation of Christ, was he not adding sin to sin, and was not his sin such that Christ might indeed pity but could not pardon, unless indeed He were to come from heaven and be crucified again?   But even then Christ would be unfaithful to His own threatenings, and besides, the Bible stated that there remained " no more sacrifice for sin," so that settled it against him. Was there a God or no?   Were the Scriptures a fable?   Was Paul himself an arch deceiver?   What was the use of striving to be saved, if he were already a chosen vessel, predestined of the Father?   And if he were *not* elected by sovereign grace, might he not as well leave off his efforts to be saved?   The devil had him there, and he was at his wit's end.   These perplexities would go on for years, leading to such

after all, was but filthy rags. He knew not Christ nor grace, nor faith, nor the new birth, and had he died then, his state would have been "most fearful." "I wanted perfect righteousness to present me without fault before God, and this righteousness was nowhere to be found, but in the person of Jesus Christ." "Sometimes I should lie under great guilt for sin, even crushed to the ground therewith, and then the Lord would show me the death of Christ; yea, and so sprinkle my conscience with His blood that I should find, and that before I was aware, that in that conscience where but just now did reign and rage the law, even there would rest and abide the peace and love of God through Christ." "Yea, I saw that the justice of God and my sinful soul could embrace and kiss each other through this blood." "Now could I look from myself to Him, and should reckon that all those graces of God that were green in me were yet but like those cracked groats and fourpence halfpennies that rich men carry in their purses, when their gold is in their trunks at home! Oh, I saw my gold was in my trunk at home! In Christ my Lord and Saviour! Now Christ was all; all my wisdom, all my righteousness, all my sanctification, and all my redemption." "Now was I as one awakened out of some troublesome sleep and dream, and listening to this heavenly sentence, ye are 'justified freely by His grace, through the redemption that is in Christ Jesus.' It was as if I heard it thus expounded to me: 'Sinner, thou thinkest that because of thy sins and infirmities I cannot save thy soul, but behold My Son is by Me, and upon Him I look, and not on thee, and will deal with thee according as I am pleased with Him.' At this I was greatly lightened in my mind, and made to understand that God could justify a sinner at any time; it was but His looking on Christ and imputing His benefits to us, and the work was forthwith done."

Thus did those great truths of Scripture cheer Bunyan's soul, and "spangle in his eyes." They did for him what they did for Wesley a century later, brought him "a very great softness and tenderness of heart," so that he was "ready to swoon for solid joy and peace." Formerly, it was all he could do to free himself from those fetters of sin which were as "clogs to a bird's foot." Now he found it as difficult to get his mind from heaven to earth, as it had once been hard to soar from earth to heaven. That blessed Scripture, Heb. xii. 22, 23, so held him that "he could scarce lie in bed for joy and peace and triumph through Christ." For, great though his sin had been, it was no more, compared to the blood of Christ, "than this little clot or stone before me is to this vast and wide field that here I see."

" Of all tears they are the best that are made by
the blood of Christ, and of all joy that is the sweetest
that is mixed with mourning over Christ. Oh, it is
a goodly thing to be on our knees with Christ in our
arms before God! I trust I know something of
these things."

So, after long buffetings, and many tackings to
and fro, and wrestlings with cross currents and
opposing winds, this sorely battered vessel reached
at last the haven where it would be. Bunyan's
experience abounded in those extremes of despair and
rapture to which this type of piety is peculiarly
exposed. It would be idle to deny that Andrewes'
piety, for example, was much more tranquil and unruffled than that of Bunyan. The bishop's wide
learning and extensive studies, his broad outlook
upon the world and lifelong acquaintance with the
teaching and discipline of a great historic Church,
saved him from those torments to which poor
Bunyan was subjected, through his private interpretation of a maze of Scripture texts. We should
never forget, in comparing the two, that, while the
Bishop of Winchester was so erudite that Fuller
could say of him that " some conceive that he might,
if then living, almost have served as an interpreter-
general at the confusion of tongues," [1] Bunyan, alas,

[1] *Church History,* XI. i. 46.

had little on his shelf but the Bible, Luther on *Galatians*, Foxe's *Book of Martyrs*, and those excellent manuals which his wife brought him as her dowry, *The Practice of Piety*, and *The Plain Man's Pathway to Heaven*. Yet may it not be claimed that Bunyan's piety, if narrower and more troubled, was the robuster of the two? His experiences may have been less measured and even, but they abounded more in the extremes of rapture and despair. Andrewes was not unlike the elder brother in the parable, to whom the Father said, "Son, thou art ever with me, and all that I have is thine." Bunyan rather resembled the poor demoniac boy, of whom we are told that he had a spirit which tare him and cast him into the fire and into the water to destroy him, but which was subject at the last to the gentle rule of Christ. And who shall measure the joy of that deliverance, when "Jesus took him by the hand, and lifted him up, and he arose?"

In the beautiful stained glass window presented to Westminster Abbey some years ago by Mr. Childs of Philadelphia, there are enshrined the figures of two of our representative English saints, George Herbert and WILLIAM COWPER. The men thus brought together had much in common. Both of them were Anglicans, and both were poets. Each had a sensitive and gentle shyness of nature, mingled with a strain of quaint humour. Each of them elected to flee the world and burn his quiet taper in solitude apart. Yet in spiritual outlook and experience they were essentially diverse, and they admirably reflect the two main currents of religious feeling which divide our national life. The one, that is to say, is a characteristic example of the institutional, or ecclesiastical, type of piety in England, the other of the evangelical.

Herbert was the spiritual child of Andrewes and of Laud. Cowper, on the other hand, was the child of John Wesley in religious matters, and desired only to determine the bounds of his habitation by the proximity of an evangelical clergyman. It is true that he wrote hymns, and Olney hymns. But they are not hymns that bring before us Olney Church, except in so far as they reflect the views of the Olney vicar, who was the Rev. John Newton, a pirate saved by grace. Herbert so loved the church at Bemerton, and its sacramental seasons, that he must needs clip the very lines of his poems to the shape of the holy altar or a pair of Easter wings. But one has the impression that Cowper was more at home in Lord Dartmouth's drawing-room prayer-meetings at the Great House, Olney, than even in the communion services of the parish church, and that he loved the solitary devotions of his own garden summer-house best of all.

> "The calm retreat, the silent shade,
>   With prayer and praise agree ;
> And seem by Thy sweet bounty made
>   For those who follow Thee.
>
> There, if Thy Spirit touch the soul,
>   And grace her mean abode,
> Oh ! with what peace, and joy, and love,
>   She communes with her God !
>
> There like the nightingale she pours
>   Her solitary lays ;
> Nor asks a witness of her song,
>   Nor thirsts for human praise.
>
> Author and guardian of my life,
>   Sweet source of light divine,
> And—all harmonious names in one—
>   My Saviour ! Thou art mine !"[1]

In Cowper the peculiar experiences of the evangelical were heightened by the delicate temperament of the poet.   He had a sense of sin greatly in excess of his relative sinfulness, and one which was acutely aggravated by his constitutional tendency to insanity.   It led him to believe that he was " damned below Judas," and the worst of sinners.   Passages in the Bible and even in Beaumont and Fletcher pointed the finger at his incorrigible wickedness. He heard voices in his dreams which told him he was doomed.   *Actum est de te, periisti.*   He accused

---

[1] *Olney Hymns*, No. xlvii. " Retirement."

himself of "a hellish spirit of rancorous reproach and blasphemy against His Maker," and could write, "I am like a slug or a snail that has fallen into a deep well. Oh, merciful God! what a Tophet of pollution is the human soul! and wherein do we differ from the devils, unless Thy grace prevent us?"[1]

From this condition Cowper was delivered by the grace of the Lord Jesus Christ, in a manner which vividly recalls St. Augustine's experience in the little garden in Milan. In the grounds of the "Collegium Insanorum" at St. Albans, where he was undergoing medical treatment for his derangement, he found a Bible which had been laid on the seat purposely to restore him. It opened at the third chapter of the Epistle to the Romans, and the twenty-fifth verse: "Whom God hath set forth to be a propitiation through faith in His blood, to declare His righteousness for the remission of sins that are past, through the forbearance of God." "Immediately I received strength to believe, and the full beams of the Sun of Righteousness shone upon me. I saw the sufficiency of the atonement He had made, my pardon sealed in His blood, and all the fulness and completeness of His justification. In a moment I believed and received the gospel."[2]

[1] T. Wright, *Life of Cowper*, pp. 96, 106, 115, 206, 220, 391.
[2] See Cowper's *Memoir*.

The reaction from blackest despair to transcendent happiness was complete and inexpressible.

> "All at once my chains were broken,
>   From my feet my fetters fell,
>   And that word in pity spoken,
>   Snatched me from the gates of Hell.
>   Grace divine, how sweet the sound,
>   Sweet the grace that I have found." [1]

It was natural that these experiences should deeply colour Cowper's theological creed, and make him, what he has become, the most pensive and tender exponent in our poetry of distinctively evangelical faith and doctrine.   Herbert was like that happy swallow, so envied of the Psalmist, that built her tranquil nest and reared her young, even by the altar of the Lord of Hosts.   Cowper, on the other hand, was like the timorous dove that escaped with beating heart out of the fowler's snare.   In one of his letters he has told us that the doctrines which were the very life of his soul and the soul of all His happiness were these, "that Jesus is a present Saviour from the guilt of sin by His most precious blood, and from the power of it by His Spirit; that, corrupt and wretched in ourselves, in Him, and in Him only, we are complete; that, being united to Jesus by a lively faith, we have a solid and

[1] *Song of Mercy and of Judgment.*

eternal interest in His obedience and sufferings, to
justify us before the face of our heavenly Father ;
and that all this inestimable treasure, the earnest
of which is in grace, and its consummation in glory,
is given, freely given to us of God ; in short, that
He hath opened the kingdom of heaven to all
believers.   These are the truths which, by the grace
of God shall ever be dearer to me than life itself ;
shall ever be placed next my heart, as the throne
whereon the Saviour Himself shall sit, to sway all
its motions, and reduce that world of iniquity and
rebellion to a state of filial and affectionate obedience to the will of the Most Holy." [1]

When Cowper turned these doctrines into verse
for the edification of the little prayer-meeting
which assembled in Lord Dartmouth's Great House
at Olney, he was not always successful, as the following extract may perhaps show :—

> "Jesus ! whose blood so freely streamed
>   To satisfy the law's demand,
> By Thee from guilt and wrath redeemed,
>   Before the Father's face I stand.
>
> To reconcile offending man,
>   Make Justice drop her angry rod ;
> What creature could have formed the plan,
>   Or who fulfil it but a God?

---

[1] *Correspondence* (ed. Wright), vol. i. p. 88, March 11, 1767.

No drop remains of all the curse,
    For wretches who deserved the whole;
No arrows dipt in wrath to pierce
    The guilty but returning soul.

Peace by such means so dearly bought
    What rebel could have hoped to see?
Peace, by his injured Sovereign wrought,
    His Sovereign fastened to a tree.

Now, Lord, Thy feeble worm prepare!
    For strife with earth and hell begins;
Confirm and gird me for the war;
    They hate the soul that hates the sins.

Let them in horrid league agree!
    They may assault, they may distress;
But cannot quench thy love to me,
    Nor rob me of the Lord my peace." [1]

These lines are bad, but they are no worse than many of Keble's. They only show that crude evangelicalism is no more fitted than crude ecclesiasticism to be expressed through the medium of lyric verse. Yet Cowper could extract the most exquisite strains of piety from his theological creed, as Keble from his. The High Churchman gave to the Universal Church such beautiful hymns as those beginning, 'Blest are the pure in heart'; 'O timely happy, timely wise'; 'There is a book who runs may read'; 'Sun of my soul, Thou Saviour dear!' But the Evangelical has contributed others which are no

[1] *Olney Hymns*, No. v. "Jehovah Shalom."

less favourites, 'Oh for a closer walk with God';
'Jesus, where'er Thy people meet'; 'God moves in
a mysterious way'; 'Sometimes a light surprises';
and that most pleading and tender expression
of the evangelical spirit, a hymn made doubly
precious when we remember how it was wrung out
of the experience of him who wrote it :—

> "Hark, my soul! it is the Lord ;
> 'Tis thy Saviour, hear His word ;
> Jesus speaks, and speaks to thee ;
> 'Say, poor sinner, lovest thou Me ?
>
> 'I delivered thee when bound,
> And, when bleeding, healed thy wound ;
> Sought thee wandering, set thee right,
> Turned thy darkness into light.
>
> 'Can a woman's tender care
> Cease toward the child she bare ?
> Yes, she may forgetful be,
> Yet will I remember thee.'
>
> .   .   .   .   .
>
> Lord, it is my chief complaint
> That my love is weak and faint ;
> Yet I love Thee and adore,—
> Oh ! for grace to love Thee more ! " [1]

In Bunyan we see evangelicalism at work in
moulding the tough strong men who won for us
the great battle of our freedom in Church and State.
In Wesley it becomes the inspirer of missionary
propaganda and philanthropic zeal.   In Cowper

[1] *Olney Hymns*, No. xviii. "Lovest thou Me ? "

it shows itself compatible with cultured simplicity, and retirement, and domestic peace. If
any one has the impression that evangelical piety
is bound up with harsh bigotry, moroseness, a
narrow and intolerant fanaticism, let him picture
to himself the scene in Orchard Side, Olney, where
a middle-aged bachelor, ripe scholar, and sensitive
droll poet is fondling hares; or drawing dabchicks;
or sitting in a summer greenhouse that is hung with
"an awning of mats," listening to the birds; or
reading aloud to two married ladies *The Diverting
History of John Gilpin*; or writing the most gay
and frolicsome letters that were ever penned. Nowhere is evangelical piety more attractively or
typically itself than in the quiet smiling happiness
of this cheerful home, where life flowed onwards as
smoothly and tranquilly and gently as the waters
of the peaceful Ouse by which it stood.

> "Now stir the fire, and close the shutters fast,
> Let fall the curtains, wheel the sofa round,
> And while the bubbling and loud hissing urn
> Throws up a steamy column, and the cups
> That cheer but not inebriate, wait on each,
> So let us welcome peaceful evening in."[1]

Yet it would be quite a mistake to associate
Cowper's piety with simpering old-maidishness and

[1] *The Task*, Bk. iv.

whimsical domesticities. His was one of the most masculine minds in the England of his day, and he could write with robust vigour, as well as pleasant wit, on behalf of the great causes of philanthropic and religious progress, of which evangelicalism was then the champion. When the fashionable world of literary London took to reading *The Task*, being weary of Pope's *Iliad* and *Rape of the Lock*, and attracted by this new poet's shy and sportive gaiety, as well as his vivid and fresh descriptions of life and nature, they found to their surprise that, ere they were aware of it, he had made them blush for shame at the prevailing vices of the ballroom and the card-table, imbued them with Whig sentiments about the fall of the Bastille, the government of India, the abolition of slavery, and the reform of debtor's prisons, and even almost inoculated them with the principles of evangelical religion![1] Cowper carried the inspiration of evangelicalism, and the humanitarian reforms which went with it, into circles which would have nothing to do with Wesley,

---

[1] "My sole drift," he wrote in 1781, shortly before the publication of his first volume, "is to be useful; a point which, however, I know I should in vain aim at, unless I could be likewise entertaining. I have therefore fixed these two strings to my bow; and by the help of both have done my best to send my arrow to the mark. My readers will hardly have begun to laugh before they will be called upon to correct that levity, and peruse me with a more serious air." (*Correspondence*, vol. i. p. 368, October 19, 1781.)

and would have scornfully repudiated Wilberforce and the Earl of Shaftesbury. "If debtors are no longer imprisoned, if India is no longer oppressed, if public schools are no longer places of barbarism and terror, if slaves are free, and animals protected from cruelty both by opinion and by law, our gratitude must not forget that Cowper pleaded for them all in what was the most popular poem of its day."[1]

It is a very tragic circumstance that the latter part of Cowper's life was darkened by religious melancholy, and its sun set behind clouds of impenetrable gloom. Whereas Herbert soared to heaven as in a chariot of fire, with his viol in his hand and songs of angels on his lips, Cowper had to plunge through the dark and icy waters of religious mania to reach the Happy Isles. "I feel unutterable despair," were almost the last words uttered by poor Cowper in this world. It is a strange and pathetic spectacle. "The poet who, of all English artists, has written the noblest hymns for depth of religious feeling and loveliness of quiet style; whose life was blameless as the water-lilies which he loved, and the way of life of which on silent streams he made his own; whose heart

---

[1] J. C. Bailey, Introduction to edition of Cowper's *Poems*, 1905, p. li.

9

breathed the sweetest air of natural piety and yet could sympathize with the supersenuous world in which Madame Guyon lived, died in ghastly hopelessness, refusing comfort to the last." [1]   Such facts as these make us thankful beyond measure for the words of the Apostle John, " If our heart condemn us, God is greater than our heart, and knoweth all things."   There is probably no happier spirit now among the saints made perfect, than the poet who thought himself engulfed in the lowest hell.   Certain it is that while Cowper's gloom vexed only himself and a few loving friends who gathered round him, his beautiful and pensive faith, like bruised spikenard, has been charged with the fragrance of joy and comfort to millions of sad souls in distress.

"O poets, from a maniac's tongue was poured the deathless singing !
O Christians, at your cross of hope a hopeless hand was clinging.
O man, this man in brotherhood your weary hearts beguiling,
Groaned inly while he taught you peace, and died while ye were smiling." [2]

III

The evangelical type of piety, like every other, has the defects of its qualities.   In the first place, it

---

[1] Stopford Brooke, *Theology in the English Poets*, p. 68.
[2] E. B. Browning, *Cowper's Grave*.

is in danger of being characterized by a certain intellectual and imaginative narrowness of outlook upon life. In exaggerated evangelicalism the moral element in religion, its aspect of strict rigour, is given solitary and overwhelming prominence. What may be termed its more genial or æsthetic side is treated as of no account. Transcendence ignores immanence, Hebraism supplants Hellenism, and the beauty of holiness can find no room for the holiness of beauty. Intensity is purchased at the price of breadth. Devotion to what ought to be frowns on all kindly interest in that which is, and the prophet, the evangelist, the censor, and the apostle impatiently elbow out of their rights the artist, the poet, the architect, and the musician.

There can be no doubt that the evangelical witness in this respect has a sound theological and philosophic basis. When it comes to a question of emphasis or priority, the moral must have precedence of the imaginative, the spiritual of the merely artistic. Art may assist morals but it is itself non-moral, and easily becomes the vehicle of the immoral and the vicious. Indeed, Plato himself proposed to banish from his ideal republic music, the most spiritual and least gross of all the arts, because of its enervating and relaxing qualities. An impartial survey of the history of the world would probably lead to the conclusion that, whereas great art has often flourished in periods of moral laxity and social cruelty and corruption, the symbolism of art has been either rude and simple or altogether absent in periods of great moral and spiritual awakening. By a dim but sure instinct the puritan or evangelical of every age has been aware of this. He has felt it to be his supreme business to remodel and reconstruct the world, turn it upside down, rather than simply represent its fair ideal forms or graceful aspects. He has recognized that, whereas the goal of all art is æsthetic enjoyment and contemplative calm, religion demands that the will be exercised even more than the feelings, and affirms that

"Calm's not life's crown, though calm is well."[1]

The pleasures, therefore, which the evangelical has naturally sought have been the pleasures of hope rather than the pleasures of the imagination. He has realized that no art can ever represent the things he is conversant with, inasmuch as they transcend all that the eye sees or the ear hears. He has profoundly distrusted and feared that facile and egoistic kind of peace in which the imagination indeed is satisfied, but the conscience is neither condemned nor reconciled. And he has been possessed

[1] Matthew Arnold, *Youth and Calm.*

by the conviction that the chief end of man is to glorify God and enjoy Him for ever, rather than to rest tranquilly in the contemplation of His works.

The protest of evangelicalism, then, has its deeply rooted justification in our religious nature. Morality demands theism, while art has many affinities with pantheism. The former leans always to the transcendence, the latter very often to the immanence, of God. Art's supreme delight is not in the moral drift of things, but in their fleeting and variegated expression ; not in what they ought to be, but in what they are. The sphere in which it moves is one in which questions of sin, conscience, and salvation are alien and remote problems. It is no friend to an austere uncompromising severance of form and matter, sense and spirit, good and evil, but loves to detect a pre-established harmony and eternal correspondence in things, in the subtle interplay and fusion of plastic symbolism, in the flying lights and shadows that cross the face of nature and of human life. What are all these but so many entrancing aspects of the manifold wisdom and character of God,

> " Workings of one mind, features
> Of the same face, blossoms upon one tree,
> Characters of the great Apocalypse,
> The types and symbols of Eternity,
> Of first, and last, and midst, and without end." [1]

---

[1] Wordsworth, *The Simplon Pass.*

The spirit of the moralist is very different. His watchwords are sin, righteousness, redemption, and a new creation. Where the one talks of taste as the supreme arbiter, the other must bow before "God's secretary, Conscience."[1] The former thinks in terms of light and shade, perfect and imperfect; the latter in terms of right and wrong, good and evil, sin and holiness. It is possible we shall never fully reconcile these differing tendencies. There is one glory of Hebraism and another of Hellenism. Renaissance and Reformation are not the same glory. The one rejoices in statues as expressions of the divine. The other, mindful of the second commandment, impatiently discards them. The one gives us Phidias, Raphael, the builders of the cathedrals. The other, Moses, Mohammed, Savonarola, and John Knox. Thus one star differeth from another star in glory.

The remembrance of these things will explain much that may seem strange in our national religious history. On the one hand there have been evangelicals in abundance who have shown a genuine devotion to culture, refinement, and the politer arts. Cromwell saved the Raphael Cartoons for the nation and set up two organs in the great hall of Hampton Court. Colonel Hutchinson was not only a perfect gentleman, as well as a Puritan and a Baptist, but

[1] Milton, *The Reason of Church Government.*

he was also a distinguished virtuoso and art collector besides, and both himself played excellently well on the viol and spent thousands of pounds on the choicest paintings, sculptures, and engravings. Bunyan, for all his spiritual intensity, was no enemy of the lighter side of life, and has given us in the *Pilgrim's Progress* attractive pictures of Prudence playing on "a pair of excellent Virginals," and of Christiana discoursing on the viol and Mercy on the lute while Mr. Ready-to-halt danced. "True, he could not dance without one Crutch in his hand, but I promise you he footed it well. Also the Girl was to be commended, for she answered the Musick handsomely." Milton, too, we remember, had no quarrel with the stage or the Muses either, and always counted himself the friend of

> "Quips, and cranks, and wanton wiles,
> Nods, and becks, and wreathed smiles
> Such as hang on Hebe's cheek,
> And love to live in dimple sleek;
> Sport that wrinkled Care derides,
> And Laughter holding both his sides."[1]

Cowper was the most fastidious and elegant poet of his day, and Lord Dartmouth, of whom he could write with somewhat questionable taste the well-known lines:

> "We boast some rich ones whom the gospel sways,
> And one that wears a coronet and prays,"[2]

---

[1] *L'Allegro.*　　　　[2] *Truth*, line 377.

was so completely and on all points the fine gentleman, that Richardson is reported to have said, " he
would have realized his own idea of Sir Charles
Grandison, if he had not been a Methodist." [1]

Yet, while these and innumerable other instances
might be adduced, it is nevertheless true that a
marked indifference to culture has been a characteristic of the evangelical type of piety in its intenser
forms. The story of the Methodist local preacher
who was presented with a copy of Euclid by a well-
wisher desirous of assisting his educational progress,
but who returned it with the remark that " he
could not see anything of Christ in the book," may
well illustrate this tendency to one-sidedness. The
man who is hurrying forward in his pilgrimage to
eternity can only regard with pity and with wonder
those who would have him dally in such arbours of
art or literature as would divert him even for a
moment from his tremendous quest. It is this
which explains the iconoclasm of the Puritans.
When zealous and strict sectaries of the baser sort
set out to smash windows and deface statues and
tombs in the parish churches, they were but
voicing, perhaps a little too loudly, the needful
ethical protest of the rising evangelical conscious-

[1] Abbey and Overton, *The English Church in the Eighteenth
Century*, ed. 1887, p. 398.

ness of the seventeenth century. It was the moral
in man claiming sovereignty over the artistic, and
no doubt doing it to excess. But such over-emphasis
was the result of a reaction, and was only to be
expected. Men whose aim in life it is to raise to
God's honour a temple of living stones are apt to
look with suspicion, and even with dislike, on overmuch attention to things graven with art or man's
device, as symbols of the divine. Having a zeal
for the kingdom of the saints and the heavenly
Jerusalem, they cannot away with stage plays or a
hobby for collecting pictures.[1] Jehovah, who is a
jealous God, must on no account demean Himself
to make way for the Nine Muses in men's esteem.
Hours devoted to artistic, literary, or other worldly
pursuits, what are they but so much time wasted, if
they do not directly lead to the saving of the soul?
Thus William Law believed that every playhouse
was the abode of Satan, just as every church was the
dwelling-place of God. Newton, the well-known
evangelical hymn-writer, professed that " nothing
had surprised or even grieved him more " than the

---

[1] "I hate to see Christian men hang up abominable Popish
things, as they sometimes do, because they happen to be works of
art. Burn every one of such artful works, whether prints or paintings. I would take the hammer and administer it with iconoclastic
zeal on all images and pictures of saints and virgins and the like,
which do but tempt men to idolatry." (C. H. Spurgeon, *Sermons*,
No. 1233.)

news of his friend Cowper's growing fondness for novel-reading; and when he heard that he was translating Homer he doubted if he was in his right mind, and added, "I knew the time when he would no more have attempted it than he would to translate the history of Jack the Giant Killer into Greek."[1] Even Wesley objected to some statues at Stourton, saying, "I cannot admire the images of devils, and we know that the gods of the heathen are but devils"; and when he heard of art treasures being collected in the British Museum, he only remarked, "What account will a man give to the Judge of quick and dead for a life spent in collecting all these?"[2]

There can be no doubt that this one-sidedness is a grave defect.   There is no reason in the world why ethics should push out æsthetics, or why an absorption in the moral and spiritual aspects of life should render us incapable of appreciating its artistic and imaginative aspects.   Jesus both loved the lily and was faithful to the Cross.[3]   Doubtless, as William Law has remarked, a man crossing a river on a tight-

[1] Quoted by J. C. Bailey, Introduction to Cowper's *Poems*, p. xix.
[2] *Journal*, 1776, 1781.
[3] It is true that Jesus took a religious rather than an artistic interest in Nature, and He referred to birds and flowers chiefly as illustrations of the divine providence.   Yet the æsthetic point of view was not wholly absent.   "Solomon in all his glory was not arrayed like one of these."

rope ought not to be curious about wearing silver slippers, nor will he be much concerned with the colour of the waves. But is that breathless, palpitating figure, poised on a swaying thread 'twixt earth and heaven, to be taken as the only adequate representation of the Christian life ? Are we to hear only of Kedar's tents, and the Vale of Baca, and never of the green pastures and the fountains of still waters ? Surely not. God hath given us all things richly to enjoy, and whatsoever things are lovely ought ever to engage a Christian's thoughts. It may be that the moral and the imaginative, the evangelical and the artistic aspects of our nature will never fully understand one another. But at least they may fulfil complementary functions, and dwell side by side. And if the evangelist feels that he has a far grander mission in life than to give the glowing visions of his soul a merely artistic or imaginative expression, at least he may do the artist the unconscious service of imparting to life itself that high seriousness and inward spiritual nobility which can alone make art vital in the generation following.

The influences on which we have just been dwelling, unbalanced moralism, suspicion of culture and the fine arts, and narrowness of intellectual and imaginative outlook, readily produce that morbid, harsh, illiberal type of character which we recognize in fanaticism. If the world be divided into the elect and the reprobate, the saved and the unsaved, it needs but a step and men will entertain the belief that Shakespeare is a lost soul in hell, and that there is more hope of salvation for a soundly converted Fijian than for the saintliest Roman Cardinal.[1] The sweetest characters are assured that the most unselfish of good works will avail them nothing, but that they are under the ban of God's wrath and curse if they are not conscious of having an interest, as it is called, in the merits of Christ's sufferings, and a share in His salvation.   Well-meaning and amiable men of the world are condemned in one formula with the most hardened sinners, for not having had that particular experience of the work of grace which is the one thing needful.   Blithe and happy children are scowled on in their play as being radically evil,[2] and those who differ from the saints in matters of theology are composedly consigned to eternal torments.

It is hardly possible to exaggerate the religious gloom and misery for which these views have been

---

[1] Note M.

[2] "The method I take to convince the Indians that we are sinners by nature is to lead them to an observation of their little children, how they will appear in a rage, fight and strike their mothers, before they are able to speak or walk." (D. Brainerd, *Journal*, First Appendix.)

and still are responsible. The surest signs of conversion to holiness of life have been thought to be sobs and groans and agonizing cries.[1] Laughter has been tabooed, the most winsome and innocent amusements sternly suppressed, and even young children of the Eternal Father enjoined to pass the time of their sojourning here in *fear*. Dancing, card-playing, theatre-going, social hilarity and diversion, however light-hearted and pure in character, have been met with sour looks and stern denunciations, and bear-baiting objected to, not so much, as Macaulay hinted, because it gave pain to the bear, as because it gave pleasure to the spectator. Here, for example, is how a contemporary writer satirized the Puritans. In his eyes they were

> " A Sect, whose chief Devotion lies
>   In odd, perverse Antipathies ;
>   In falling out with that or this,
>   And finding somewhat still amiss :
>   More peevish, cross, and splenatick,
>   Than Dog distract, or Monkey sick :
>   That with more Care keep Holy-day
>   The wrong, than others the right way :
>   Compound for Sins, they are inclined to,
>   By damning those they have no mind to :
>   Still so perverse and opposite,
>   As if they worshipp'd God for spight,

---

[1] "Cuifs of later times, wha held the notion
    That sullen gloom was sterling, true devotion."
                              BURNS, *The Brigs of Ayr*.

Rather than fail they will defie
That which they love most tenderly;
Quarrel with *Minc'd Pies*, and disparage
Their best and dearest Friend *Plum Porridge*;
Fat *Pig* and *Goose* it selfe oppose,
And blaspheme *Custard* through the *Nose*." [1]

There is too much evidence to allow us to believe that this humorous description is in any way exaggerated or overdrawn. Newton could not endure that Cowper should wear a green coat and become an archer. Wesley held it sinful for a woman to wear gold ornaments or a gaudy attire. Whitefield declared that dancers pleased the devil at every step, and innumerable other instances of evangelical moroseness and bigotry might be adduced.[2] But a precise strictness of this kind, if it were to be widely insisted on, would bring the lightest diversions and most innocent gaieties of life under the terrific ban of *lèse-majesté*, and lay a heavy weight on sinking shoulders which neither we nor our fathers should be able to bear. The rigours of Puritanism led by a sure reaction to the riotings and drunkenness, the chambering and wantonness of the Restoration, and it is impossible for a too highly strung moralism long to maintain its hold on human nature. We

[1] Samuel Butler, *Hudibras*, Canto I.
[2] See Swift, *Tale of a Tub*; Fielding, *Joseph Andrews*, bk. i. ch. xvii. ; Sydney Smith, *Works*, vol. i. p. 95 ; Lecky, *History of England*, vol. ii. p. 589.

the seventeenth and eighteenth centuries, and our whole English character and history are the better because they have been born. They have contributed the more solid and enduring elements to our national strength, and they entered a much needed protest against the frivolity and licence of the age in which they lived. Yet have they not also left behind them a plentiful crop of mischievous tradition, sabbatarian gloom, pedantic strictness, and hysterical excitement, in religion, which we could very well do without? It must sorrowfully be confessed that this type of piety has persistently placed an embargo on the innocent pleasures of the people, and some of the most cheerful gaieties of human life. It has clouded over the blue sky of God's love with earthly and uncalled-for religious terrors. It has tortured gentle and placid natures, that could not persuade themselves that they had undergone any special supernatural change, with the belief that they were obdurate, and in danger of hell-fire, or else that their day of grace was passed, and that they had committed the unpardonable sin. It has also been a fruitful source of mental and physical disorders and religious mania. Well may one who has had bitter experience of its tyranny bring the following most grave charges against it. "After my long experience, after my patience and forbearance, I have surely the right to protest against the untruth that the evangelical religion, or any religion in a violent form, is a wholesome or valuable or desirable adjunct to human life. It divides heart from heart. It sets up a vain, chimerical ideal, in the barren pursuit of which all the tender, indulgent affections, all the genial play of life, all the exquisite pleasures and soft resignations of the body, all that enlarges and calms the soul, are exchanged for what is harsh, and void, and negative. It encourages a stern and ignorant spirit of condemnation; it throws altogether out of gear the healthy movement of the conscience; it invents virtues which are sterile and cruel; it invents sins which are no sins at all, but which darken the heaven of innocent joy with futile elements of remorse. There is something horrible in the fanaticism which can do nothing with this pathetic and fugitive existence of ours but treat it as if it were the uncomfortable ante-chamber to a palace which no one has explored, and of the plan of which we know absolutely nothing."[1]

[1] E. Gosse, *Father and Son*, p. 367. Compare the words of Lord Dalgarno, in Scott's *Fortunes of Nigel*, chap. xii.: "Credit me, the Puritans who object to us the follies and frailties incident to human nature, have themselves the vices of absolute devils, privy malice and backbiting hypocrisy, and spiritual pride in all its presumption."

10

The evangelical type of piety, further, while it is strong in its moral and missionary aspects, is apt to be weak on its æsthetic side, the side of ordered worship. Nonconformity, especially, is poor in all outward and visible representation of the great doctrines of the gospel, and in symbols of the corporate unity and continuity of the Church of Christ. When a Romanist or High Anglican goes to worship he knows that he will be borne forthwith into the main stream and current of catholic tradition. The great verities of the faith will be rehearsed publicly before his eyes at every service with due solemnity and a becoming attention to emphasis and proportion. Before a single word has been spoken or an act has been performed he will be bathed in an atmosphere of hushed grandeur and mystery and high religious awe. The ceremonies in which he will take part will be the most seemly and reverential which art and symbolism can suggest. He will learn to approach God in the chastest and most appropriate language which lips can utter, in prayers which are comprehensive and universal while they are pointed and concise, and which are inexpressibly endeared to him through historical association and countless memories of childhood. Above all, he can be certain that the divine sacrifice of the Cross will be elevated before him for his adoring wonder, and round it will be grouped the appropriate confessions, praises, and petitions of the Holy Catholic Church throughout the world. In that sublime drama he will be made to feel that something has been actually done in the spirit world, and not simply talked about in this world, inasmuch as God has there and then positively come into His temple, and quickened His faithful worshippers by His energizing will. These influences play about him to deliver him from the vagaries and idiosyncrasies of a too personal and capricious piety, and school him to the pattern of the great historic saintliness as it is shown him on the mount by Mother Church.

These things mean much to the typical Anglican worshipper, but there is little or no guarantee that any of them will be provided in a Nonconformist service. There is no *certainty* that the breadth and universality of Christian aspiration will be expressed; or the word of divine forgiveness definitely and authoritatively spoken; or the largeness, beauty, and proportion of Christian truth adequately and impressively displayed; or even the sacrifice of Christ so much as mentioned. Nonconformist worship has its own peculiar excellences. By sheer simplicity and directness it may rise to heights of spiritual sublimity and devout fervour which leave the tawdry pomp of an elaborate and gorgeous

of brass, or its equivalent, and the groan also, should such be necessary? Evangelical and especially Nonconformist piety would surely be richer if in its worship there were more impressive symbolism and outward order, more catholicity, more quiet resting-places for secret silent prayer and adoring wonder, more things to look at and to do that are beautiful in themselves, and symbolically suggestive of the great verities of the faith, and the communion of the Holy Catholic Church throughout the world.

Lastly, this type of piety is exposed to special perils on its moral side. Evangelicalism, throughout its entire history, has been haunted by the dark shadow of antinomianism. The doctrine of justification by faith is of itself an emancipating doctrine, one which, firmly grasped, is a sure safeguard of the purest morality, and leads to the loftiest conceptions of life and duty. Weakly apprehended, however, it may be the reverse, through becoming a cloak for the greatest evils, and so setting up faith as a substitute for good works as to encourage the vicious notion that a man may go on sinning that grace may the more abound. Colonel Hutchinson tells us of one Chadwick, a voluble and crafty man, with a great reputation for sanctity, who " kept up his credit with the godly, cutting his hair and

taking up a form of godliness the better to deceive."
Yet he was a knave at heart, and "among other
villainies which he practised, he was a libidinous
goat, for which his wife, they say, paid him with
making him a cuckold."[1] Wesley himself had the
greatest difficulty in repressing these excesses, and
on one occasion had a dialogue with an antinomian
teacher in Birmingham, who assured him that,
"being no longer under the law, he was the heir of
all things, and had the right to take whatever
goods and lie with whatever woman he pleased."[2]
These extravagances have been especially associated
with the Calvinistic doctrine of final perseverance,
in its cruder travesties, and the belief that the
elect must surely be saved, no matter how they
conducted themselves, inasmuch as no one was able
to pluck them out of their Father's hand. But it
has its roots in that proneness to self-deception
which is characteristic of human nature generally,
and is compatible with many different systems of
belief. "The head," wrote William Law once to
John Wesley, "can as easily amuse itself with a
living and justifying faith in the blood of Jesus
as with any other notion; and the heart which
you suppose to be a place of security, as being

---

[1] Colonel Hutchinson's *Memoirs*.
[2] Lecky, *History of England*, vol. ii. p. 596.

the seat of self-love, is more deceitful than the head."[1] Evangelicalism has its own way of becoming unethical, even as sacerdotalism has. In the one case a man will take refuge in an efficacious sacrament, in the other he will find shelter in some doctrine of Christ's atonement, if he wishes to be easy about personal religion. In either case religion has become vicarious, and something external to the soul has been substituted for its own inward travail of moral earnestness and spiritual faith.

There are two characteristic streams of influence now noticeable in the modern world which may be regarded as somewhat unfavourable to the evangelical type of piety. The first is that which flows in the direction of monism. The thoughts of many are moving insensibly away from the old dualism towards a less transcendent and more immanent view of God. They are becoming dissatisfied with some of the more anthropomorphic conceptions of the past which represented God as a supremely holy Person over-against the world, who felt a special interest in this particular planet, and stooped down to save it at the moral crisis of its history, by a unique, final, and miraculous revelation of Himself in the person of His Son. Instead of this, God is coming to be regarded, in

[1] Tyerman, *Life of Wesley*, vol. i. p. 187.

many quarters, as an ineffable and mysterious Source of physical and psychic energy, who can scarcely be described as personal, for He aims at no final and consistent goal, but sweeps all worlds along with Him in a kind of creative evolution, towards ends which may be dimly guessed in the ever-growing complexity of the Universal Life. Thus by a kind of new Copernicanism many are loosening their hold on the old anthropocentric and geocentric systems, and are gravitating in the direction of a more theocentric or cosmocentric view of reality. As a result of this more biological and evolutionary conception of the universe they find themselves less and less at home in a system of thought and belief which assumes a fundamental inner cleavage and disruption in things, with two opposing kingdoms of sin and grace, hell and heaven, nature and the supernatural, and a reconciliation effected by atoning sufferings which are of the nature of a special intervention or redemptive miracle, and do not organically arise out of the previous trend of things.

The second adverse influence is that of collectivism, which reacts strongly against the old individualism in religion, as in everything else. The strong current of interest at the present day flows in the direction of social rather than of personal reform, through the working of communistic forces which aim rather at humanitarian than at religious ends. Accompanying this is a marked concentration of energy and thought upon this present world. Remote questions as to the final spiritual destiny of the individual soul are pushed aside in view of the immediate problems of industry and unemployment, the socialization of all life, the production and distribution of wealth, the organization of society, and the inauguration of an eagerly anticipated earthly paradise. The modern man tackles such problems generally with a joyous earnestness and enthusiastic self-confidence which are worthy of all praise. He is absorbed in the fascinating task of exploiting and subduing the whole earth, and of harnessing the newly discovered forces of the modern world to the car of civilization, in the hope that he may thus expand man's secular activities in all directions, and immensely enhance the value of human life. For the most part he feels himself quite equal to all these tasks, and is convinced that he will find satisfaction in them when they are accomplished, without reference either to the judgments or to the rewards of another world.[1]

[1] "Civilized society should be raised above mere material animal distress;—little else is needed for its reformation; there are plenty of social forces which make for good, if they had a chance of

With these two forces evangelicalism has to-day to reckon, and it is inevitable that they must profoundly influence its appeal. No doubt, as a result, its emphasis may be modified, its phraseology altered, its more anthropomorphic and mythological elements pruned away. But evangelicalism is old enough, and strong enough, to survive these changes, and it is too suited to the needs of the human heart to be long discredited. The day of its victory will come again. Periods of shallow thinking or of eager practical absorption in outward tasks may for a time draw off men's interest from the problems of the soul's inner life, its freedom, its responsibility, its rift of sin and guilt and doubt and fear. But it is inevitable that these problems must return from the periphery to which they have in some cases been banished, and resume their former commanding place in the very centre and citadel of man's concern. Starving in the midst of plenty, impotent in the face of tasks he would fain achieve, torn by an inner contradiction between good and evil, homeless within a world of chance and change, and in dire need of mercy and a new creation, he will learn again, as he has learned before, that if he is to

acting, if they were not too heavily handicapped,—humanity itself is good enough if given a chance." (Sir Oliver Lodge, *Reason and Belief*, pp. 52, 53.)

attain even to the fruition of his own ideal it must be through a deliverance wrought for him by a higher Power. He will realize, in the collapse of all things, that he can rise to a new and eternal spiritual life only through the convulsive leap of faith and the strong descending arm of a divine Helper, who sends from on high and takes him and draws him out of the great waters. He will find also, in the future as in the past, that even humanitarian reforms are best advanced by religious means; that religious reforms are deepest as well as most fruitful and abiding when they make the individual rather than the common salvation their chief concern; and that nothing so changes the individual, and raises him to the power of a transfigured life, as the gospel which condemns him, and humbles him, and frees him from his sin, by the love of the Holy Father, acting through the grace of the Redeeming Son, and the life-renewing power of the Eternal Spirit.

THE MYSTICAL TYPE

I

MYSTICISM, as a form of piety, is the passion and hunger of the soul for immediacy of access to the Father, and the all-satisfying vision of His eternal glory. Its chief characteristic is a kind of spiritual impatience with all that is merely mediate or imperfect in our knowledge of the Deity, and an ardour of desire to rise from the shadow to the substance, from illusion to reality, from the symbol to the thing symbolized, and to attain to the intoxicating blessedness of perfect union with the divine, so that self and the world shall be forgot in our absorption in the Father, and God Himself shall "cease to be an object, and shall become an experience."[1] Why should we be content with the husk, when we may have the kernel? Why should we dwell on the letter, when we may have the spirit? Why seek God in the heaven above or on the earth

[1] A. S. Pringle-Pattison, "Mysticism," in *Ency. Brit.* (ed. 1911).

a divine simultaneity, through our identification with Him who is the Alpha and the Omega, the Beginning and the End, the Being who is, and who was, and who is to come. Thankfully would the soul press through the dereliction of a rich night and a good darkness if it might thus reach the ineffable glory in which God dwells. On its religious side, mysticism is the desire for the perfect fruition of human life, through the beatific vision of Him "in whose presence is fulness of joy, and at whose right hand there are pleasures for evermore." Mysticism is eager to taste and see that God is good. It seeks to experience the peace that passes all understanding, the peace in which all whispered doubts, and obstinate questionings, and restless cravings have for ever folded their wings as in a quiet nest, inasmuch as we have at last become partakers of the divine nature, and faith and hope themselves have become lost in love. On its moral side, mysticism aspires not merely to an ethical harmony of the human with the divine will, through obedience and submission, but even to an ineffable union through ecstasy and absorption. Thus only can the warring passions of the soul be reconciled, life's jarring discords be resolved into a psalm, evil itself be seen to be no substance but a shadow only, 'might be,' 'should be,' 'ought to be' become merged in 'is,' and the end of all ethics be realized at last.

The goal of mysticism, in a word, is that blessed mood spoken of by the poet Wordsworth which "transcends the imperfect offices of praise and prayer,"[1] and in which thought itself expires in blessedness and love. In such moments, to ask anything of God were as superfluous as to thank Him for that which we receive. We do not think of ourselves as separate from Him at all. The soul is caught up into God, as Elias into heaven in a chariot of fire. We are what we are because God realizes Himself in us. Our love to God becomes part of that infinite love by which God loves Himself in Christ the Eternal Son from the foundation of the world. Love the gift, Love the giver, and Love the receiver of the gift, are one and the same Love. For as the iron glows with a fervent heat when laid within the furnace, and as the air can be fully saturated with summer sunshine, so may the soul of man be radiated through and through with the love of God. We live, yet not we, but Christ liveth in us, made one with us in nature, even as He is in the Father and the Father in Him. Mysticism, in short, is the search for the timeless and universal element

[1] Wordsworth, *The Excursion*, i. 216.

in experience, that true heaven of the soul which is not more there than here, not more then than now, but which is just life itself, life at its best, life more abundant, the life which is everywhere and always eternal because it is divine, and consists in the knowledge of God, and of Jesus Christ His Son, whom He hath sent.   Indeed, we may borrow Shelley's fine metaphor, and say that it is the task of mysticism, as of death, to shatter life's dome of many-coloured glass, and to enable us to gaze with unveiled face on the pure and dazzling radiance of eternity which it obscures.[1]

It is the conviction of every mystic that a life so lost and swallowed up in God is not in the least impoverished, but rather immeasurably enhanced. If a larger personality becomes ours in proportion as we identify ourselves socially with our fellow-men, how infinitely may we be enriched if, through a complete renunciation, we are emptied of self altogether, and are filled with all the fulness of the love of God!   When we are in such a state, life's covering and deceiving mask is unaccountably removed, the key to its mystery is found.   Doubts and fears vanish, and the irksomeness of duty disappears.   No commandment is now grievous to us and no task difficult.   Christ's yoke is seen to be

[1] Note N.

easy and His burden light, for He Himself dwells in us with a love that beareth all things, empowering us to do what He commands. Work has become rest, and the wilderness and solitary place have blossomed as the rose. God's ways are ways of pleasantness and all His paths are peace. We *run* the way of His commandments with delight, because He has enlarged our heart.

Mysticism in the Christian Church has a long history and a noble ancestry. It is built on a foundation of many prophets, such as Wordsworth and Coleridge, More and Cudworth, Boehme and Tauler, Eckhart and Plotinus, Paul and John, Jesus Christ Himself being the chief corner-stone of all the noblest elements in its structure. Philosophically it has affinities with the systems of Schleiermacher, Schelling, Fichte, Berkeley, and Spinoza, and every form of Platonism. If the universe be the living garment and vesture of the Eternal, the ever-changing shadow of His unchanging substance, the expression of His heart and mind and will in terms of time and space, where should we look for the surest tokens of His presence, if not in the heart and mind and will of the child whom He has made, all whose highest strivings are those of God Himself? Mysticism holds that in the human soul there dwells a germ of the divine nature, God being, as it were, the life-principle of the soul, even as the soul is the life-principle of the body. Man at his noblest is the temple of the Lord, and his spirit is as a quiet shrine in which the candle of the Lord for ever burns, a flicker of smoking flax to be in no wise quenched by Him who kindled it, and who lighteth every man coming into the world.

Were there no such divine spark or image of God in man, no element of identity underlying every difference, communion or fellowship between the two would be impossible. It is by virtue of a fundamental and inalienable kinship that we can speak to God at all, as to a Father and a Friend. On this essential groundwork of the soul the mystics fix. From every logical attempt to demonstrate the being or personality of God they turn to that instinctive mutual embrace in which it is impossible to say whether we apprehend God or are apprehended by Him. The soul's confidence in the rationality of its own moral and spiritual intuitions plumbs deeper than all the ratiocinations of the speculative intellect. Granted that we cannot by searching find out God, it is still open to us to feel after Him, if haply we may find Him. The mystic does not attempt to prove rationally the existence of God, on the plea that that which is the ground of all our consciousness cannot properly be made its object. As well might the dolphin ask, Can there be a sea? or the eagle put the question, Can there be an atmosphere? *In God we live and move and have our being.* It is the aim of mysticism to push back beyond our existential judgments to value judgments and transcendental feeling. It seeks to rise above the reflective distinctions of will, feeling, intellect, memory, and imagination in consciousness, and reach that primal, diffused, undifferentiated awareness, or intuition of the whole, in which consciousness first emerges, and which, it is believed, is the soul's most immediate contact with the divine. Conceptual thinking is not yet. Even the rudimentary distinctions of self and not-self are still submerged, and divine realities are apprehended, not in modes which the understanding can define, but in high dream and solemn vision, in trances, in raptures, and in exaltations. In modern phrase, there is a " more " of consciousness continuous with our own. Beneath the superficial current of our conscious ideas there is the ever-flowing stream of our subconscious life, itself in tidal communication with incalculable floods and inflowings of the divine. It is the belief of the mystics that we may dive and plunge freely into these depths and come up braced. The artist derives his pictures from thence, and the poet his visions. The musician goes there for his melodies, the saint for his triumphs and his dreams. Our highest achievements and most axiomatic truths are ever those in which the conscious self plays but the smallest part. They come to us and well up within us rather than proceed from us. We do not measure them, they measure and judge us. They are to be reported simply rather than reasoned out, and even in the reporting memory itself may fail.[1] Experience holds more than knowledge can explain, and things may be given which are not inferred. Only let the over-assertive will refrain from meddling, let passion subside and the tension of thinking be relaxed, let us learn to lean back absolutely and to breathe deeply, resigning ourselves to Him in whom we live and move, and the tides of universal being will flow through us unimpeded, our soul will be cleansed and reinvigorated with spiritual life, and we shall find that we are greater than we know.

It will be seen from the above that it is the tendency of mysticism to emphasize, sometimes to over-emphasize, the importance of feeling in religion. The best mystics, it is true, recognize that mind,

---

[1] "Appressando sè al suo disire,
Nostro intelletto si profonda tanto,
Che retro la memoria non può ire."

DANTE, *Paradiso*, i. 7.

Christ. Saint Teresa, for example, the greatest of
the Spanish mystics, was a fervent Catholic, while
William Cowper, who lovingly translated Madame
Guyon into verse, was an ardent Evangelical. Its
underlying assumptions, however, will be seen to be
in marked contrast to those of the two types we
have already been considering. The difference
between mysticism and evangelicalism, like most
fundamental differences in theology, runs back to
varying conceptions of man and God, as well as of
the relation that exists between them. Evangelicalism approaches God chiefly through the conscience,
and is impressed by the awful contrast between man
and his Maker. Mysticism approaches God more
through the spiritual imagination, and is struck
rather by their likeness and possible identity. The
one emphasizes more the transcendent aspect of
God, and leans to deism. It conceives God as a
holy and sublime Person, other and larger than
ourselves, who *confronts* us both in creation and
in redemption. The other emphasizes rather the
immanent aspect of God, and inclines to pantheism.
It conceives Him as the ground and centre of our
being, One who *dwells in us* as the divine Lodger
and Sustainer of the soul. The former, therefore,
speaks much of sin and grace, corruption and holiness, a fallen man and a redeeming God, the need of

a mediator and of a new creation. The latter speaks
of man's kinship with God by virtue of the divine
image already imprinted upon his constitution, and
of the clearing of that image further by spiritual
illumination. The gospel of mysticism is an
"eternal gospel," grounded on universal being,
rather than a "historical gospel," tied to the
happenings of time. Its God is the Absolute, the
All, the One, the Uncreated Light, rather than the
Holy One of Israel, who is plenteous in redemption,
and of purer eyes than to behold iniquity.

These fundamental differences reveal themselves
markedly in the place that is assigned to Jesus
Christ. Evangelicalism takes a transcendental if
not a transactional view of Christ. He is the heavenly
man who 1900 years ago descended to humanity from
another sphere, in order that on Calvary He might
accomplish a mighty deed for the salvation of the
world. The view of mysticism is more immanent
and subjective. Christ is the indwelling principle of
divine life in nature and the soul. Calvary is not
so much an objective, cosmic deliverance as it is the
historic dramatization of something that must take
place within ourselves, the dying to sin and self and
the living to righteousness and God.[1] Mysticism

---

[1] "The Incarnation . . . is a perpetual Cosmic and personal
process. It is an everlasting bringing forth, in the universe and

proper has no love for externality in religion, or for
any "finished work" in the doctrine of salvation.
Its true economy of redemption is within, and the
only reconciliation it values is that by which Christ,
the indwelling Spirit, purifies and subdues the soul,
turning it from fear to faith and from hate to
love, and infusing harmony and peace and power.
Mysticism, that is to say, takes more kindly to
sanctification than to justification. It is more at
home in *Ephesians* than in *Romans*, and is prone to
dwell on the Incarnation rather than on the Atonement. It will have nothing to do with imputed
righteousness or a forensic salvation, and looks upon
redemption not as a historic deed *changing* the
nature of things, but rather as a cosmic process
involved in the nature of things. The Christ it
loves is the Christ in us rather than the Christ for
us ; the Christ of to-day and of eternity, rather than
the Christ of 1900 years ago ; the Christ who is
indwelling Logos to lead things on, rather than
a heavenly deliverer to put things right; a
universal principle rather than the Son of Mary.
Christ, in short, is the Lord, the Spirit. The

also in the individual ascending soul, of the divine and perfect
Life, the pure character of God, of which the one historical life
dramatized the essential constituents." (E. Underhill, *Mysticism*,
p. 141.)

historic details of His life, what He did in Galilee or suffered on Calvary, are matters of subordinate interest, since what happened only once cannot be all-important. The main things to be concerned with are spiritual tendencies and laws, and the redemptive process of Christ's birth, life, death, and resurrection in the souls of believers.

But if the mystical type of piety differs essentially from the evangelical, it no less widely diverges from the sacerdotal. It is true that there are many devout mystics to be found among the priestly faiths, more, perhaps, than among the non-priestly. The mystic, as a rule, is something of a poet, and is likely to love symbols, sacraments, and a speaking ritual. There is something in the æsthetic pageantry of sacerdotal worship, the exclusion of irrelevancies, the solemn and ordered rehearsal of the great verities of the faith, the multifarious appeal to eye and ear, which is psychologically more calculated than the bare forms of puritanism to arouse the sensibilities of the mystical worshipper.[1] But it is nevertheless true that, though the mystic may avail himself of priestly aids in his devotions, the sources of his piety are not priestly. Mysticism is subjective, Catholicism objective. Mysticism exalts the inner light above outward authority and finds everything

[1] Note O.

sacramental. Catholicism would subordinate inspiration to authority and revelation, and make only a group of things sacramental. It demands in its votaries a *fides implicita*, and cannot approve the *ignis fatuus* of an inner light which may lead to any swamp, and may even contain within itself dangerous possibilities of combustion and ecclesiastical reformation. Hence its tendency is to tolerate and suspect mysticism rather than to welcome it. " The mystic," says Professor Harnack, " who does not become a Catholic is a dilettante."[1] Yet there are elements in true mysticism which a sacerdotal Church can never assimilate. A system whose first principle is that spiritual things must be spiritually discerned and can be appropriated only by the leap of the heart and the grasp of a living faith, can never be on wholly friendly terms with a system which teaches that grace may be communicated by sacraments *ex opere operato*, and that a spiritual efficacy resides in rites, priesthoods, and ceremonies in themselves.[2]

The religion of a mystic, that is to say, rests no

---

[1] Quoted by W. R. Inge, *Christian Mysticism*, p. 345.

[2] It is significant that Eckhart, Tauler, Suso, Molinos, Fenelon, and Madame Guyon were all of them persecuted by the Roman Catholic Church, chiefly because their influence tended to withdraw the faithful from rosaries and the mass to merely mental prayer.

more on an external authoritative church, than on an external authoritative book, but only on internal authoritative spirit. Its springs and sanctions are within.[1] Rosaries, sacraments, ceremonies may be an aid to faith. So may windows, candles, pillars, architectural beauty of design. So may the written Word. But the object for which these things exist is that they may themselves be superseded, and the soul discard these aids, and spread its wings, and soar as with the lark to heaven's dawn. The true mystic leans neither to an external church nor to an external dogma, for he knows of greener pastures and stiller waters than these. In his attitude to all ceremonies and observances he is as one who feels that since that which is perfect is come, that which is in part may be done away. Of the heaven to which he aspires it may indeed be said, "There is no temple therein." The symbol itself has become superseded by the thing symbolized. He himself is his own priest and penetrates to the Holy of Holies of the inner shrine, a shrine in which there are "no mystical half-lights but the mystical half-lights of faith, no windows but the many-hued windows of hope, no arches but the vault of love."[2]

---

[1] "Mystics are the only thoroughgoing empiricists." (J. Royce.)
[2] James Lane Allen, *The Choir Invisible*, chap. xviii.

It remains that we should briefly study the means by which this goal of mysticism is to be attained. Mystics, speaking generally, may be divided into three groups. There are those in the first place who, like Crashaw or Faber, are most readily lifted to mystical states by the rites and ceremonies of the Church. Nothing so moves them to awe and gratitude and wonder as the cross, the bread, the wine, and those other emblems of the divine mysteries which the Church, our nursing Mother, so plentifully provides. Such never feel that these things are fetters to the spirit, or in any way hinder the immediacy of their access to God. Rather they regard them as divinely appointed media of communion, designed both to express and effectuate our union with the Father. Thus Cardinal Newman writes : "The Catholic Church allows no image of any sort, material or immaterial, no dogmatic symbol, no rite, no sacrament, no saint, not even the Blessed Virgin herself, to come between the soul and its Creator. It is face to face, *solus cum solo*, in all matters between man and his God." [1]

Others, like Blake, Coleridge, and Wordsworth, are nature-mystics, who agree that some symbols are helpful and even necessary if we would commune

[1] *Apologia pro Vita Sua*, ed. 1890, p. 195.

with the divine, but who feel that those of the
Church are altogether too limited and too poor.
"The symbolism of the mysteries," writes Galen,[1]
"is more obscure than that of nature," and we are
reminded by John Smith, the Cambridge Platonist,
that "it is a drowsy and muddy spirit of superstition which is fain to set some idol at its elbow,
something that may jog it and put it in mind of
God. Whereas true religion never finds itself out
of the infinite sphere of the Divinity. . . . And
seeing God hath never thrown the world from
Himself, but runs through all created essence, con-
taining the archetypal ideas of all things in Himself,
a soul that is truly godlike, and hath its inward
senses affected with sweet relishes of divine goodness, cannot but everywhere behold itself in the
midst of that glorious unbounded Being who is
indivisibly everywhere."[2] Such nature mystics believe that "the invisible things of God are clearly
seen from the things that are made," and would
worship in a temple not made with hands, a shrine
whose aisles are the meadows, whose vault is the
infinite blue, whose organ tones are those of the
wind and of the sea. To these the earth, the grass,
the clouds may be sacramental, as truly signs and

---

[1] Quoted by W. R. Inge, *Christian Mysticism*, p. 306.
[2] *Select Discourses*, p. 441.

symbols as bread and wine may be of the real presence of Him,

> " Whose dwelling is the light of setting suns,
> And the round ocean and the living air,
> And the blue sky, and in the mind of man." [1]

Only let the human spirit be rightly attuned to the divine, and the whole framework of things becomes a shadow of the Eternal, the creation itself groaneth and travaileth in pain, waiting for the revealing of the sons of God, and every common object is index of a life, an animating soul, which circulates everlastingly from star to flower.[2]

Finally, we have a group of quietists, like Fox, Barclay, and the Quakers, who as a rule eschew symbolism, and seek by the interior road of devotion to gain their goal, " sinking into themselves from thought to thought." In some cases this attitude may be due to an absence of the artistic temperament, but oftener it arises from a feeling that symbolism, while it helps little, hinders much. The symbolism of the Catholic Church is too meretricious ; the symbolism of Nature is too diffuse ; the the highest and best things cannot be symbolized at all. For to whom will ye liken God, or what likeness will ye compare unto Him ? Better flee altogether from the material to the spiritual, from

---

[1] Wordsworth, *Tintern Abbey*.   [2] Note P.

the outer to the inner, from the glare to the twilight, and bow with patient expectation before the Christ, who lies hid within the silent chamber of the heart.[1] Or, if he is to be discovered elsewhere than in the secret place, the cup of cold water is as likely to contain Him as the altar chalice. He dwells in the bread given to the hungry man as much as in the sacred wafer to which a whole congregation bows. Too much ceremony with God is surely an impertinence. It introduces overpoliteness between Father and son, where true love would be eager and run to an embrace. Even when most expressive, symbols have after all but a secondary purpose to fulfil. Their use is either to lead up to some better thing, and to prepare us by means of things earthly for the vision of things heavenly, or else to reduce the sublime verities of the faith to material symbolic forms, that so they may be conveyed to many minds. But they are necessarily inadequate to the highest experiences themselves, in which there is no speech nor language, but only things unutterable. Climb high and leave the world, then make of the unruffled heart a mountain pool. That is the proper mirror to reflect the stars.[2]

There is one underlying principle which is common

[1] Note Q.   [2] Note R.

to all these groups, and it is this that, whatever be the means adopted by each, the end is to bring the soul itself into unison with the divine. God is not far from any one of us. Yet the veil which hides Him from us can be rent by no ceremony nor by any creed, but only by our purifying ourselves even as He is pure. Were we but like Him we should see Him as He is, for nothing veils Him from us but the evil will. To attain to this inner likeness is the goal of mysticism. It aims at tuning the æolian harp of the human soul to such a pitch of harmony with the mind and will of God that to every chord He strikes our own will vibrate, making a blissful and harmonious response, like the music of the spheres.

Nor is this end easily to be attained. It is a mistake to suppose that mystics, by virtue of a specially favourable temperament, can swoon at the outset into the infinite, or attain their quest at a bound. Mystics are under no delusion on this point. They know quite well that faith, patience, struggle are required in the pursuit of the divine life, and that if the mirror of the soul is to reflect the heavens, it must be diligently polished and cleansed from all filthiness of the flesh and spirit. Or, to vary the metaphor, if God's holy hill is to be ascended, and we are to view the landscape o'er from that lofty height, we shall have need of clean hands and a pure heart and much toil in climbing. Those who have gained these altitudes tell us of three stages that have to be passed in the ascent. First, there is the tedious and difficult *purgative* stage, in which the will is chiefly exercised. Here we learn to deny self, to die unto the world, and by hard and painful discipline in penitence, obedience, and self-control, to acquire the first practical and social virtues of the Christian life. It is the irksome steady pull of the beginning of our journey, ere we have quite got into our stride, so to speak, or found our wind. Then comes the *illuminative* stage in which progress is transferred from the outer to the inner life. Obedience has become more instinctive and ingrained; the effort of self-compulsion is scarcely now required; habits which formerly had to be imposed upon us have become second nature; life's outward tasks are more easily and mechanically performed; and the soul is set free for its own spiritual advance. At the same time the horizon widens, the air becomes more invigorating, and we see with admiring wonder, as in an expanding landscape, the breadth, the glory, and the wisdom of the purposes of God. Finally, we reach the *unitive* or contemplative stage of perfect love. We are at the summit then. The panting of the earlier stage has passed away, for laws have become lyrics now, and statutes songs. The zest even of the middle stage is left behind, with its ever-enlarging prospects, for now faith itself is transcended, and has become lost in sight. Only love remains, a love that, having suffused the discursive intellect and wholly governed the will, is free now to direct the entire being to Him who is its source and yet its goal. Earth with its cares is beneath us and only heaven above, while all life's devious pathways converge to where we stand. The soul has reached its goal of sabbatic rest. On such a mount of transfiguration the end of all our striving is attained. Lost in adoring wonder and in blissful love we behold the King in His beauty, and the land of far distances opens to our gaze.

II

About the middle of the seventeenth century, when England was echoing loud to the clash of arms, a certain HENRY VAUGHAN might have been seen, guiding his little pony in meditative mood by the banks of the river Usk, in Brecknockshire. He was a man of honourable family and ancient lineage, of whom little is known save what we are told of him by Anthony à Wood, namely, that he " made his first entry into Jesus College in Mich. term, 1638, aged 17 years ; where spending two years or more in logicals under a noted tutor, he was taken thence and designed by his father for the obtaining some knowledge in the municipal laws at London. But soon after, the civil war beginning, to the horror of all good men, he was sent for home, followed the pleasant paths of poetry and philology, became noted for his ingenuity, and published several specimens thereof, of which his *Olor Iscanus* was most valued. Afterwards applying his mind to the study of physic, he became at length eminent in his own county for the practice thereof, and was esteemed by scholars an ingenious person, but proud and humorous." Vaughan had written some amorous verses in his youth in imitation of John Donne. But a severe illness and the chance reading of the poems of that holy man George Herbert entirely changed the current of his life, and determined him to flee the wanton muse and live seriously. Accordingly, he set himself to follow the calling of a physician in the wilds of Southern Wales, holding commerce with heaven the while through the beauties of nature, and recording his pious musings in religious verse.

Vaughan had the temperament of a genuine mystic. It is true, he was in all things an orthodox and devoted member of the Church of England, but his inspiration deserted him, as it did Wordsworth,

when he essayed to write poetry on definitely ecclesiastical subjects, and only returned when he strayed
from everything that was formal or external in his
devotions, and relied more on intuition than on
authority for his religious faith.

> " For yet, as angels in some brighter dreams
> 　　Call to the soul when man doth sleep,
> So some strange thoughts transcend our wonted themes,
> 　　And into glory peep." [1]

Vaughan has not that playful and never-failing
delight in the chaste outward accessories of worship
which marked his predecessor Herbert, making him
so excellent an example of sacerdotal piety.　His
chief characteristic as a religious poet is his haunting visionary sense of the immediacy, nearness, and
reality of the spiritual world.　He writes as one
who is restless with the feeling that he is but "a
tenant here," [2] an exile and a wanderer from his
proper country.　Life is a pilgrimage from eternity
to eternity, but cheered by flying messages from our
relinquished home.　This world is but the shadowed
semblance of a dream.　A veil of clouds keeps us
here in a dim twilight, hiding that blaze of glory
in which God dwells, and suffering but faint and
intermittent gleams to radiate through.　Our peace

---

[1] *They are all gone into the world of light.*
[2] *The Match.*

and rest are to be found elsewhere than here, in the happy isles of the blest for which we yearn. "Celestial natures still aspire for home."[1] Vaughan in his *Silex Scintillans* is love-sick with a celestial longing to be "all soul."[2] He desires to rise above the mists and fogs of earth and see without a glass, to be delivered from this "world of thrall," and to find his liberty and joy in being hid in God.

> "O that Thy spirit would so strongly move me:
>   That Thou wert pleas'd to shed Thy grace so far
>   As to make man all pure love, flesh a star!
>   A star that would ne'er set, but ever rise,
>   So rise and run as to outrun these skies."[3]

Some of Vaughan's lines about the supersensuous world are very haunting. How felicitious, for example, is his comparison of eternity to a clock with ever-revolving hands but no figures to its dial.

> "Heav'n
> Is a plain watch, and without figures winds
> All ages up; Who drew this circle even
>   He fills it; days and hours are blinds."[4]

For the most part, however, after the manner of St. John, he likens eternity to light, mystic, un-created, supernatural, above the brightness of the sun, to which men might soar on wings of holy

---

[1] *The Palm-Tree.*   [2] *Cheerfulness.*
[3] *Love-sick.*   [4] *The Evening Watch.*

faith, did they not prefer their drear abode of grots
and caves of earth.

> " I saw Eternity the other night,
>   Like a great ring of pure and endless light,
>   All calm, as it was bright;
>   And round beneath it, Time in hours, days, years,
>   Driv'n by the spheres,
>   Like a vast shadow mov'd; in which the world
>   And all her train were hurl'd." [1]

This strange unearthly whiteness, as of the transfiguration robes of Christ's own glory, gleams with
a silver lustre through Vaughan's religious verse.
He loves to speak of white stars, white flowers,
white thrones, white wings, white garments of the
saints.   He feels sure that Christ's coming as the
Church's Bridegroom will take place in the radiance
of the dawn, when darksome night is past,[2] and he
looks back longingly to the time when, in the
Garden of Eden, man was

> "All naked, innocent, and bright,
>   And intimate with Heav'n, as light." [3]

At the same time he has the true mystic's love of
darkness, as the quencher of garish day and the
abode of all deep mystery and spiritual delight.
How melodiously sweet, and soothing as cool

[1] *The World.*   [2] *The Dawning.*   [3] *Ascension Hymn.*

hand laid upon fevered brow, are the well-known lines.

> " Dear Night! the world's defeat;
> The stop to busy fools; care's check and curb;
> The day of spirits; my soul's calm retreat
>   Which none disturb!
> Christ's progress, and His prayer-time;
> The hours to which high Heaven doth chime.
>
>   God's silent, searching flight;
> When my Lord's head is fill'd with dew, and all
> His locks are wet with the clear drops of night;
>   His still, soft call;
> His knocking-time; the soul's dumb watch,
> When spirits their fair kindred catch.
>
>   There is in God—some say—
> A deep, but dazzling darkness; as men here
> Say it is late and dusky, because they
>   See not all clear.
> O for that Night! where I in Him
> Might live invisible and dim!" [1]

What is this but Boehme's " divine darkness," the darkness which lies coiled in the abyss of Deity itself, the eternal Nay which dwells even in the heart of the everlasting Yea? "The mystic," says Dionysius, "must leave behind all things both in the sensible and in the intelligible worlds, till he enters into the darkness of nescience which is truly mystical." [2]

The way to reach these visions is by the inward

[1] *The Night.*   [2] See W. R. Inge, *Christian Mysticism*, p. 109.

road of purity and meditation and detachment from
the world.

> "A sweet self-privacy in a right soul
> Outruns the earth, and lines the utmost pole." [1]

These come to the soul in dreams rather than
waking thoughts, or in those silent and blessed
reveries when the senses sleep, and the spirit flies
released to its proper sphere, and "odours and
myrrh and balm o'errun the heart" like a rich
flood.[2] The only explanation which Vaughan can
give of these mystic states is the Platonic one, that
they are shadowy recollections of an earlier and
diviner state of being. In one of his characteristic
poems he describes how, having searched in vain
for a solution of life's mystery in nature, he proceeds to study man, only to find that he himself
is made up of echoes, hieroglyphics, and broken
letters of a departed glory.[3] He returns to the
same subject in *The Retreat*, where the soul's
wistful reminiscence of its home in God is depicted
in lines that are said to have suggested to Wordsworth his *Ode on the Intimations of Immortality*.

> "Happy those early days, when I
> Shin'd in my angel-infancy !
> Before I understood this place
> Appointed for my second race,

---

[1] *Rules and Lessons.*   [2] *Mount of Olives.*   [3] *Vanity of Spirit.*

Or taught my soul to fancy ought
But a white, celestial thought;
When yet I had not walk'd above
A mile or two from my first love,
And looking back—at that short space—
Could see a glimpse of His bright face;
When on some gilded cloud, or flow'r,
My gazing soul would dwell an hour,
And in those weaker glories spy
Some shadows of eternity;
Before I taught my tongue to wound
My conscience with a sinful sound,
Or had a black art to dispense
A several sin to ev'ry sense,
But felt through all this fleshly dress
Bright shoots of everlastingness."

It is this reverence for the elusive presence of
the Eternal in early life which explains Vaughan's
marked affection for little children. Their angels,
he believes, circle the throne of God " in a bright
ring," and, he adds, it is the " young sweet mirth "
of their glad hosannas that joins both heaven and
earth in joyful harmony.[1]   Ardently Vaughan
yearns to return to the " white designs " of childhood and its harmless thoughts, and so " by mere
playing go to heaven."   But it may not be.

"I cannot reach it; and my striving eye
Dazzles at it, as at eternity.

   .   .   .

An age of mysteries ! which he
Must live twice that would God's face see.

---

[1] *Palm-Sunday.*

> How do I study now, and scan
> Thee more than e'er I studied man,
> And only see through a long night
> Thy edges and thy bordering light!
> O for thy centre and midday!
> For sure that is the narrow way!"[1]

Meanwhile, if childhood's innocence is beyond us, Nature provides a ladder by which we may climb to God. Vaughan is deeply impressed by the harmony and order and obedience so constantly to be found in the outward world. Birds go to their beds betimes, flowers rise with the sun, and bees "get them home to hive."[2] Everywhere in Nature we come upon the most startling and suggestive types and symbols of things spiritual.

> "Mornings are mysteries; the first world's youth,
>   Man's resurrection, and the Future's bud
>   Shroud in their births."[3]

Does the poet overhear the crowing of the cocks in early dawn? Why then, he reflects,

> "Their magnetism works all night,
>   And dreams of Paradise and light."[4]

Does he come upon a bird singing its song merrily after a wet night? It is chirping its matins, and raising early hymns of gratitude to Providence.[5]

---

[1] *Childhood.*　　　　[2] *The Check.*
[3] *Rules and Lessons.*　　[4] *Cock-crowing.*
[5] *The Bird.*

Does his heart leap up to behold the rainbow? Then it is a message flashed from the throne of Him "who minds the covenant of All and One."[1] Vaughan is full of the Platonic conception of a soul in Nature, the thought of the music and harmony of the spheres.

> "All things here show man heaven ; waters that fall,
>   Chide, and fly up ; mists of corruptest foam
> Quit their first beds and mount ; trees, herbs, flowers, all
>   Strive upwards still, and point him the way home."[2]

But alas! man's soul is sluggish and sinks earthwards. In contrast with universal nature he either misses or ignores his true ascent and "sleeps at the ladder's foot."

> "He knows he hath a home, but scarce knows where ;
>   He says it is so far,
> That he hath quite forgot how to go there."[3]

So depressed is the sensitive poet with this universal apathy that he feels he could serve God better if he were a pearl, a rainbow, or a star,[4] and oh! that he might obey God with a calm and steadfast watchfulness and peace, as the constellations do![5] Vaughan believes that this spiritual symbolism has been impressed on Nature by the

---

[1] *The Rainbow.*
[2] *The Tempest.*
[3] *Man.*
[4] *The Pilgrimage.*
[5] *The Constellation.*

same infinite Being who flashed the interpretation thereof into the heart of man. Sitting by a water-fall, he thus reflects,

> " What sublime truths and wholesome themes
>   Lodge in thy mystical, deep streams!
>   Such as dull man can never find,
>   Unless that Spirit lead his mind,
>   Which first upon thy face did move,
>   And hatch'd all with His quickening love." [1]

Heaven would be attained could but the soul of man join tunefully, as it ought, in that "undisturbed song of pure concent" [2] which Nature sings.

> " Hark ! in what rings
> And hymning circulations the quick world
>   Awakes and sings !
>   The rising winds,
>   And falling springs,
>   Birds, beasts, all things
>   Adore Him in their kinds.
>   Thus all is hurl'd
> In sacred hymns and order ; the great chime
> And symphony of Nature. Prayer is
>   The world in tune,
>   A spirit-voice,
>   And vocal joys,
>   Whose echo is heaven's bliss." [3]

Such things, however, belong to eternity and not to time. Now we see through a glass darkly and but in part. Only when the day breaks and all

---

[1] *The Waterfall.*   [2] Milton, *At a Solemn Musick.*
[3] *The Morning Watch.*

shadows flee away shall God's unveiled glory be revealed and we be privileged to behold Him face to face.

> "Then we that here saw darkly in a glass
>   But mists and shadows pass,
> And, by their own weak shine, did search the springs
>   And course of things,
>   Shall with enlighten'd rays
>   Pierce all their ways,
>
> .   .   .   .
>
> Rove in that mighty and eternal light,
>   Where no rude shade, or night
> Shall dare approach us; we shall there no more
>   Watch stars, or pore
> Through melancholy clouds, and say
>   ' Would it were Day !'
> One everlasting Sabbath there shall run
> Without succession and without a sun." [1]

Vaughan was thus a typical example of true mysticism. He read in things seen and temporal the flying messages and gleams of the unseen and eternal, communing with the supersensuous world in the sacraments much, in nature more, in his own soul most of all.

When Charles Lamb said of SAMUEL TAYLOR COLERIDGE that he was an "archangel a little damaged," "a stranger or visitor to this world," [2] he spoke, as was his wont, that perfect and final

---

[1] *Resurrection and Immortality.*
[2] *Letters*, April 26, 1816, and March 11, 1823.

word about him which others would have toiled in
vain to find. Coleridge was a spirit which chafed
and fretted sadly against the confines of the flesh,
and never could quite fit in with the conditions
and demands of ordinary life. A heavy body and
a swift and restless mind; a constant vacilla-
tion between radiant vivacity and despondency and
sloth; an incapacity for dealing with monetary or
domestic affairs and the business of real life; a
habit of projecting vast schemes, both literary and
political, without doing anything to realize them,
of turning up late or not at all to duly announced
lectures, and of issuing magazines to subscribers at
most irregular intervals; an insatiate craving for
narcotics, that should numb the dull pains of the
body and liberate the soul to its heavenly dreams—
these were indications of a spirit pent rather than
housed in the body of mortal flesh, and tragically
ill adapted to the jars, duties, and conflicts of our
workaday world.

> " You will see Coleridge ; he who sits obscure
>   In the exceeding lustre and the pure
>   Intense irradiation of a mind
>   Which, with its own internal lightning blind,
>   Flags wearily through darkness and despair—
>   A cloud-encircled meteor of the air,
>   A hooded eagle among blinking owls." [1]

---

[1] Shelley, *Letter to Maria Gisborne.*

Most transcendental of all in Coleridge was his stream of talk, a stream that flowed for ever on, as from perennial fountains in another world. It began in his earliest years when his astonished uncle carried him, a child of ten, to declaim in taverns and coffee-houses in the neighbourhood of Threadneedle Street. It continued when he was at Christ's Hospital, and Charles Lamb listened with adoring wonder to the "inspired charity boy," who could dilate on the mysteries of Iamblichus and Plotinus. It accompanied him to Cambridge, where he recited political pamphlets to admiring undergraduates; and to Calne, where he rhapsodized by the hour in the market-place on the price of corn. Hazlitt heard the marvellous flow in a Unitarian Chapel in Shrewsbury, and tells us that the preacher launched into his subject "like an eagle dallying with the wind," and that he spoke with a voice that "rose like a stream of rich distilled perfumes." Finally, to Gillman's house in Highgate came Carlyle and Emerson and Edward Irving and many more, to sit reverently at the mountain's base, while dense clouds of metaphysics, lit up by lightning gleams, descended in ample folds from the heights above. In every case Coleridge was himself the Ancient Mariner of his own exquisite creation. He held men by his glittering eye and by his strange discourse, so that they could not choose but hear, and led them through a weird and endless labyrinth of whirling words by the clue of some golden thread of philosophic speculation—

> "From Hope and firmer Faith to perfect Love
> Attracted and absorbed ; and centred there
> God only to behold, and know, and feel,
> Till by exclusive consciousness of God
> All self-annihilated the soul shall make
> God its identity : God all in all !
> We and our Father one !" [1]

Coleridge had thus a nature apt for mysticism. It was he who first gave currency to the saying that every man is born either a Platonist or an Aristotelian, and there could be no doubt on which side his own sympathies lay.   Coleridge was himself like the æolian harp he has so well described, vibrant to all the wandering breezes of the spirit that bloweth where it listeth, and familiar with—

> "such delights
> As float to earth, permitted visitants !
> When in some hour of solemn jubilee
> The massy gates of Paradise are thrown
> Wide open, and forth come in fragments wild
> Sweet echoes of unearthly melodies,
> And odours breathed from beds of amaranth." [2]

Coleridge was early indebted to the mystics, and has recorded of such writers as Fox, Boehme,

---

[1] *Religious Musings.*   [2] *Ibid.*

Tauler, and William Law that "they contributed to keep alive the heart in the head; gave me an indistinct, yet stirring and working presentiment, that all the products of the more reflective faculty partook of death, and were as the rattling twigs and sprays in winter, into which a sap has yet to be propelled from some root to which I had not penetrated, if they were to afford my soul either food or shelter."[1] "I have little faith," he wrote, "yet am wonderfully fond of speculating on mystical themes. . . . The article of faith which is the nearest to my heart—the pure fountain of all my moral and religious feelings and comforts—is the absolute Impersonality of the Deity."[2] Coleridge openly averred that he had no interest in facts as facts, but only in those universal principles and truths by which the isolated fact must be interpreted and discerned. Facts without ideas would be mere History. Ideas without facts would be mere Philosophy. It is the blending of the two that constitutes Religion.[3] Coleridge was the chief leader of reaction against the empirical school of philosophy in this country, and the most eloquent exponent of German

---

[1] *Biographia Literaria*, chap. ix.
[2] *Letters*, 12th March 1794 and 5th December 1803. For Coleridge's later views on Mysticism, see the close of *Aids to Reflection*.
[3] *Table Talk*, 3rd and 27th December 1831, 13th July 1832.

13

Romanticism, as represented by Fichte and Schelling.
The organ by which we apprehend truth is spiritual
intuition, itself a ray of the Uncreated Light.   The
Reason is from above, the *Understanding* is from
beneath, and when the latter has groped vainly
for its object in the dark, the former can light a
match, as it were, and see it in a flash.   Yield
to the inspiration of this heavenly gleam, and
it will carry you into realms of beatific vision,
where the distinctions of subject and object are
transcended.

> " There is one Mind, one omnipresent Mind
> Omnific.   His most holy name is Love.
> Truth of subliming import ! with the which
> Who feeds and saturates his constant soul,
> He from his small particular orbit flies
> With blest outstarting !   From himself he flies,
> Stands in the sun, and with no partial gaze
> Views all creation ; and he loves it all,
> And blesses it, and calls it very good !
> This is indeed to dwell with the Most High !
> Cherubs and rapture-trembling Seraphim
> Can press no nearer to Almighty's throne." [1]

So light and airy, indeed, are the wings on which
Fichte bears his ardent disciple aloft into the realm
of the Unconditioned, that the soul even loses its
identity altogether through being absorbed in God,
and self with a small initial letter becomes Self
with a large one.

[1] *Religious Musings.*

" A sordid, solitary thing,
Mid countless brethren with a lonely heart
Through courts and cities the smooth savage roams
Feeling himself, his own low self the whole ;
When he by sacred sympathy might make
The whole one Self ! Self, that no alien knows !
Self, far diffused as Fancy's wing can travel !
Self, spreading still ! Oblivious of its own,
Yet all of all possessing ! This is Faith !" [1]

To descend from these altitudes to examine the external evidences of Christianity is not easy, and Coleridge saw no necessity for doing so. True, he both began and ended his days in the orthodox faith, and desired that his loving devotion to the Church of England might be inscribed on his tombstone. But for a great part of his life he was a convinced Unitarian, and he always continued to approach the truths of the gospel from the speculative and intuitive standpoint. Christianity is true because it "finds" us. The dogmas of the Trinity, Incarnation, and Redemption are to be credited not because they are supernaturally revealed or authoritatively promulgated or testified by miracles, but because they correspond to the necessary truths of the philosophic reason, are congruous with human nature, whether in the individual or the race, and when truly accepted and acted upon satisfy the deepest needs and

[1] *Religious Musings.*

longings of the heart.[1]   Coleridge held that our
natural powers of reason, will, and understanding
were "*pre*configured to the reception of the Christian
doctrines and promises," and even earnestly maintained that he would not abate one jot of his faith
in God's power and mercy though he were to be
convinced that the New Testament were a forgery
from beginning to end.[2]

In his attitude to the sacraments of the Church
Coleridge wavered somewhat.   He was never much
of a believer in rites and ceremonies, and in his early
years he refused to allow his children to be baptized.
In later life, however, he confessed that he "never
could attend a christening service without tears
bursting forth at the sight of the helpless infant
in the pious clergyman's arms."   Coleridge finally
subscribed to "so much of Christianity as was
common to all the churches, Catholic and Protestant, East and West, excluding the Unitarians."
As to the Quakers, he knew not what to say, since
an article on the sacraments would exclude them.
"My doubt is, whether Baptism and the Eucharist
are properly any *parts* of Christianity, or not rather
Christianity itself; the one, the initial conversion or
light, the other the sustaining and invigorating life,

[1] *Biographia Literaria*, chap. xxiv.
[2] See *Table Talk*, 28th July 1832, footnote by H. N. Coleridge.

both together the φῶς καὶ ζωή of Christianity."[1] We have here a sentence which shows Coleridge veering round from the mystical to the sacerdotal conception of Christianity. It may well explain the belief of both Thomas Carlyle and Cardinal Newman that his influence was one of the fountain streams of the Tractarian Movement.[2]

Yet Coleridge was never by temperament a sacramentarian, and his whole nature was alien from dependence on the mere customs and ceremonies of devotion. In a curiously autobiographical passage in *The Pains of Sleep* he seems to indicate that formally to engage in prayer was irksome to him, and that he preferred the mystical trance of a kind of spiritual self-magnetization.

> "Ere on my bed my limbs I lay,
> It hath not been my use to pray
> With moving lips or bended knees;
> But silently, by slow degrees,
> My spirit I to love compose,
> In humble trust mine eyelids close
> With reverential resignation,
> No wish conceived, no thought exprest,
> Only a *sense* of supplication;
> A sense o'er all my soul imprest
> That I am weak, yet not unblest,
> Since in me, round me, everywhere
> Eternal Strength and Wisdom are."

---

[1] *Table Talk*, 12th January 1834.
[2] Carlyle, *Life of Sterling*, chap. viii.; Newman, *Apologia*, ed. 1895, p. 97.

The truth is that the real home of Coleridge's worship was not the parish church, which he valued chiefly for its services to general culture,[1] and in which he was often woefully disappointed with the preaching,[2] but rather the temple of the universe, in which his expansive soul could roam at large. " I never find myself alone, within the embracement of rocks and hills . . . but my spirit careers, drives, and eddies, like a leaf in autumn; a wild activity of thoughts, imaginations, feelings, and impulses of motion rises up within me."[3] The starry night in whose awful depths twinkle those tiny sparks which are suns to other worlds; the pine-clad slopes of Chamouni, whose rainbows and blue gentians and snow-fed cataracts proclaim the living God; and the homeless winds and sea-cliff's verge of England, whither the Spirit of Liberty has fled from " Priest-craft's harpy minions "—these were the scenes among which the poet loved to bow the head, " in inward adoration of the great I AM, and of the filial WORD that reaffirmeth it from eternity to eternity. whose choral echo is the universe."[4]

In a sense, Coleridge's life was a failure. It was like some rambling prospectus of a vast projected

[1] *Biographia Literaria*, chap. xi.
[2] *Table Talk*, ed. Ashe, p. 300 ; *Fears in Solitude*, ll. 63–86.
[3] *Letters*, 14th January 1803.
[4] *Biographia Literaria*.

work never to be issued. His fatal discursiveness and procrastination, his constitutional sloth, his readiness to will anything but the immediate business of the hour—these were his undoing, and the words he used to Emerson of another were a striking characterization of himself, "The man was a chaos of truths, but he lacked the knowledge that God is a God of order."[1] Yet had he been more precise and methodical in his working, Coleridge could never have been that inspired magician we have learned to admire and love. There are some things which are seen more divinely in the pale glamour of moonlight than in the clearest sunlight. Such are ever the truths, of art, of poetry, of religion, which gleam from the wizard pages of Samuel Taylor Coleridge.

III

We may now venture on some general appraisement of the type of piety thus analysed and illustrated. Mysticism is strongly entrenched in the New Testament, especially in the writings of St. Paul and St. John. God is there set forth as Life, Love, Spirit, the Light inaccessible and full of glory, in whom is no darkness at all. He dwells in the eternal Now, counting a thousand years as if

---

[1] Emerson, *English Traits*, chap. i.

they were one day, and bearing the same relation to Abraham, Isaac, and Jacob as to ourselves.

Of this absolute and ineffable One, Christ is the Logos, or Word, the culminating expression of Himself in terms of time and space. As such He is the archetypal idea of all things, the Creator and Sustainer of the world, having a glory of His own before the world was, living before Abraham, the spiritual Rock of Israel, and the Light that lighteth every member of the human race. It is true, He did become flesh at a certain point in history, and take unto Himself the seed of Abraham. But that does not prevent His residing with all His members still, as the life of the vine permeates all its branches. He still receives a cup of cold water in the person of His poor ones. He is present wherever two or three are gathered together in His name, and will be with them all the days, even to the end of the age. During His earthly life Christ was the King of all mystics, inasmuch as the Spirit was poured without measure upon Him. He pleased not Himself but made it His meat and drink to do the Father's will. Christ stands perpetually as the mystic's goal. The things He did, He did not from Himself, but from the Spirit which dwelt within Him as a constant presence. He and the Father were one.

And as the Father dwelt in Christ, so does Christ

dwell in those who love Him.   Such are admitted to
a gnosis or knowledge of divine things which no
earthly wisdom could attain unto.   Flesh and blood
do not reveal them unto us, but only our Father
which is in heaven; and he who believeth hath the
witness of such revelations in himself.   Being pure
in heart he can see God, and needeth to be taught
of no man.   He discerns the deep things of God
which are hid from the wise and prudent, and is
entitled to judge all things, himself being judged of
none.   Such will be initiated into secrets which are
reserved for the perfect, and will know the wisdom
of God in a mystery, in ways that will seem foolish-
ness to the natural man, and through visions and
revelations catching him up to paradise and enabling
him to hear things unspeakable, which it is not law-
ful for a man to utter.

The mode by which such blessedness must be
attained is through losing our life in order to find it
again in a larger fuller self.   The whole process of
Christ's redemption must be actually repeated in the
soul.   Christ must be born in us, and we with Him
must die to sin and self, and rise again into newness
of life, till it is no longer we who live, but He who
liveth in us, to quicken our mortal bodies and to
transform us from glory to glory into His own likeness.   The final goal of all is not a merely future

judgment, for we are judged already, and have passed from death to life while we are here, but rather the attainment of the measure of the stature of the fulness of Christ.   Even now are we sons of God, but it doth not yet appear what we shall be, when, being altogether made partakers of the divine nature, and Christ dwelling wholly in our hearts through faith, we shall be strong to apprehend with all saints what is the length and breadth and height and depth of the love of Christ which passeth knowledge, and be filled with all the fulness of God.

And the honoured place which mysticism holds in the New Testament it has maintained in the history of the Church.   The true heralds of the faith and forerunners of reform are always mystics.   Again and again, when the blight of formalism or infidelity has fallen on the Church, and men's faith has grown stereotyped, and their affection cold, and the living spirit of Christianity has become bound in pedantry and ecclesiasticism, the mystic has been sent to bring release to the captive, and to open the eyes of the blind.   It has been his function to revive the spirit of religion as a fresh personal experience, and to lead men who have become parched through wandering in the wilderness of a formal externalism to the ever-satisfying fountains of the devout life.   Mystics bring poetry and romance into religion, and restore the

Some have deserved this reproach, but the slightest examination of the lives of the mystics will show that the best are altogether free from it. It is true that saints of the mystical type are, as a rule, chiefly occupied with the contemplative virtues, but that is because, in the best cases, they have mastered, not because they have neglected, those that are more practical. Was ever woman more sensible, for example, or more busy in good works, than St. Theresa, or more effectively active in the affairs of the world than St. Catherine of Siena? William Law, the mystic, was unwearied in philanthropy, and strenuously opposed the abuses of his time, and no history of political emancipation or social reform in this country could be written without continual and honourable mention being made of the Quakers. It would be surprising if it were not so, and if the dews that descend so plentifully on the mountains of God's spiritual Hermon should not do something to turn the mill-wheels in the valleys below. Who so likely to renew their strength and to exercise it aright as they who wait continually on God, and whose eyes are fastened unto the Lord, even as a maiden's unto the hand of her mistress? The truth is, that no one is so irresistible as the practical mystic. Let but Oliver Cromwell, or Colonel Gardiner, or General Gordon see visions and dream dreams in the secret place, let them then emerge and deal with the things of this world, and come to the help of the Lord against the mighty, and they will be fair as the moon, clear as the sun, and terrible as an army with banners.

The defects of mysticism, to which we now turn, relate chiefly to its philosophical presuppositions, its attitude to history and to evil, and its moral tendency in general.

The philosophical quagmire into which every form of mysticism is in danger of falling is pantheism. Anxious to flee the Scylla of dualism, it swerves and becomes a prey to the Charybdis of monism. God at all costs must not be regarded as one Spirit among many, or as some kind of supreme Personality which stands over against a multitude of other personalities. Rather He is the ground of all spirits and their final home, the one and only Being in whom personality is complete, if it can properly be affirmed even of Him, and in union with whom we are to attain our own.

The danger here is that, instead of finding our personality by this process, we lose it altogether. The line which separates self from God, subject from object, the conscious from the unconscious, may be very thin and difficult to define. But once you cross it you fall into the abyss. It is that one step which leads from all to nothing, from light to darkness, from affirmation to negation, from the sublime to the ridiculous. Goethe has said that "there is no sadder sight than the direct striving after the Unconditioned in this thoroughly conditioned world," and everything that savours of self-deification or complete *identification* with God in mysticism should at once be dismissed as the wildest of delusions. When we read in Mechthild of Hackeborn: "My soul swims in Godhead like a fish in water," or in Eckhart: "The eye by which I see God is the same as the eye by which He sees me," or in Emerson: "I am become a transparent eyeball. I am part of God,"[1] we scarce wonder at Wesley's uplifted hands and indignant ejaculation that such mysticism is "sublime nonsense, inimitable bombast, fustian not to be paralleled."[2]

The true Christian position is, not that we merge or are absorbed into the Absolute, but that we hold fellowship with the Father, as He is mediated to us through His Son Jesus Christ our Lord, and that, in all our communion with God, the Father remains personal and so do we. Our

---

[1] See these and other quotations in W. R. Inge's *Christian Mysticism*.

[2] See *Thoughts upon Jacob Boehme*, in *Works*, vol. ix. pp. 509–14.

union with God, that is to say, is not and never can be one of simple identity of substance, but is rather our relationship of perfect harmony with one another and with Him, as incorporated parts and abiding unique constituents in a spiritual kingdom of souls of which God is the life and home. Indeed, communion would be possible on no other terms. If we are to speak of love, worship, knowledge, fellowship, at all, these must involve some kind of reciprocity, a give-and-take on both sides. There must be the hunger and the Food, the desirer and the Desired. And if a point is ever reached in which the distinction between the Creator and His creatures becomes obliterated, then the religious relationship ceases, worship becomes impossible, and a quasi-pantheistic self-consciousness takes its place. The soul, like a fish out of water, must gaspingly expire. The goal of mysticism, therefore, is of necessity unrealizable by us, so long as we retain our present consciousness. A perfect union with God is unattainable in time. What shining more and more unto a perfect day may be reserved for us in another life we do not know. But in this it would be well for us to emulate the humility of Manoah, and to remember that to look upon the face of God with human faculties were only to be blasted with excess of light. Moses sought to gaze upon the glory, but it was denied him. Jacob essayed to know the name or essence of Jehovah at Peniel, and was maimed in the doing of it, although he received a blessing. And John on Patmos, when a symbolic vision was vouchsafed him of the First and the Last, whose eyes were like a flame of fire and His voice as the sound of many waters, fell at His feet as one dead. It were well, therefore, to rest satisfied with the answer given to the disciple Thomas, and when our hearts say, "Show us the Father, and it sufficeth us," to be content with so much of the excellent glory as is mirrored to our human faculties in the face of Jesus Christ. To attempt to go behind Him to the superessential One is to lose all. That perfect union with God the Father which is impossible to these earthly faculties because of their limitations we may yet rejoice in as potentially ours, and transcendently secured to us in Christ Jesus. Meanwhile we may be thankful to rest from the midday glare of the Uncreated Light in the oasis shadow of the Incarnation. "No man hath seen God at any time. The only begotten Son, which is in the bosom of the Father, He hath declared Him."

A similar peril attendant on mysticism is bound up with its attitude to history. It is a favourite contention of mystical writers that ultimate spiritual

and civilization, and possess but a relative value. Besides, the generation of the Son of God is an eternal rather than a temporal act; the Lamb of God is a Lamb slain from the foundation of the world; Christ is the same yesterday, to-day, and for ever. Mysticism believes that that which is enthroned above time may not be bound to the chariot wheels of time. God, who is the condition of the time series, cannot in any proper sense be brought within that which is but a partial reflection of Himself. If He be revealed in time at all, it must be throughout the whole process, and not by means of any one miraculous or supernatural communication vouchsafed to us at time's apex or history's central point. Even if such a communication should be regarded by us as a divine revelation, it must be so judged by virtue of some immediate religious sense within the soul to which such a revelation can appeal, some standard which is itself timeless and which values and appraises the things of time rather than is determined by them. Only a God already spiritually immanent within us could acclaim, or even recognize, a God supernaturally revealed. To pin one's faith, therefore, to any one particular event that may once have taken place in history, however important it may have been, is to anchor the soul not to the Rock of Ages, but to some

true that only by the influence of such facts upon us can these principles of judgment themselves be formed. Each is necessary to the other. Mysticism ever tends to belittle or dispense with an objective and historical Christianity altogether ; and it is in danger of forgetting that the revelation of Christ in history is something incomparably richer than anything we should ever have known apart from Him. In its love for the inward, the immediate, the abstract, the universal, it is prone to disparage the concrete, the definite, the actual, and the external ; and in its disinclination to build on any-thing that merely happened once, it is apt to set too low an estimate upon the Christ who once suffered for our sins, and the faith once for all delivered to the saints. A thoroughgoing mysticism might regard the idea of Christ or the myth of Christ as just as serviceable to humanity as the fact of Christ ; and if in any particular the recorded facts of the teaching or life of Jesus should clash with the intuitions of the mystical consciousness, it would be proper to transcend such facts altogether and disregard them. The soul might thus claim the right to dispense with the entire historico-sacra-mental scheme of things as hitherto made known to us, and arrive at the truth simply by its own inner light. The Church will always be guarded from such errors if it keeps close to the teaching of the Apostle John. No one could be more mystical than this disciple. No one has made more or better use than he of symbol, drama, and allegory, in setting forth truths that are eternal. Yet no one has insisted more firmly on the importance to the gospel of its central historic facts. The whole fabric of Christianity would gradually give way, if it could be shown that its foundation in history is insecure, or that the pillars on which it rests are laid on shifting sands.

The greatest caution is needed in dealing with the attitude of mysticism to sin. It is an essential implication of philosophical mysticism that there is no such thing as evil *sub specie aeternitatis*, and that therefore God Himself cannot be what *we* call good. He transcends all human distinctions of good and evil, and dwells in an uncreated Light which is not antithetical to darkness, in our sense, but rather includes it.[1] God's home is a realm or state of being in which all such earthly opposition is done away. Evil, therefore, is but apparent. It arises from the necessary contrasts, imperfections, and multiplicities of time, but such wavelets have no place in that sea of glass mingled with fire which constitutes eternity. All limitation is of itself metaphysical evil, and necessarily involves physical

[1] See above, p. 183.

evil, which we call suffering, as well as moral evil, which we call sin. Yet evil, in the light of eternity, is no substance, but only a shadow; no stumbling-block, but only a stepping-stone. It is the attempt of the partial to be something apart from the universal, the dead weight of nature seeking to return to chaos.[1]

The objection to this mode of thinking and speaking is that, while it may be good metaphysics, it makes very unsatisfactory ethics, and cannot be turned into a religion. It retires from the mystery of iniquity, or soars airily above it, rather than frankly faces its awful problem. It is a solution which dwells unduly on the immanence of God to the neglect of His transcendence, which offends the moral consciousness, leads to the slackening of endeavour, and commits the cardinal error of viewing the principle of evil through the mind rather than through the conscience and the will, its proper

---

[1] "To Thee there is no such thing as evil, and even to Thy creation as a whole there is not, because there is nothing beyond it that can burst in and destroy the law which Thou hast imposed upon it. In the details there are things which, because they suit not some parts, are counted evil, yet these same things suit other parts, and are good to them, and are good in themselves. And all these things which are not suitable to one another are yet suitable to the lower half of creation called earth, which has its own windy and cloudy sky of like nature with itself." (St. Augustine, *Confessions*, Bk. vii. chap. xiii.)

seat. Juliana of Norwich, praying peacefully in her cloister and anticipating the close of the cosmic process, foreshortening all history till *alpha* and *omega* meet, and viewing the confusions and contradictions of time as they are reconciled harmoniously in the perfect peace of eternity, may part her pale lips to murmur tranquilly, "Sin is behovable, but all shall be well, all shall be well, and all manner of thing shall be well." What people who are brought into close contact with slums and brothels and asylums are made to feel is that, for the present at least, all is *not* well, whatever may be the case with the future; and that, if words are to have any meaning at all, sin is just the one thing that is *not* behovable, but that, on the contrary, it is ugly, loathsome, devilish in the extreme, a thing to be slain outright, as the coiling enemy of God.

Perhaps it is impossible for us to combine these two ideas in a single act of consciousness, and we shall incline to one view or the other according as the moral or the theosophical predominates in our constitution. It would seem that while we are actually engaged in fighting with evil, we are obliged to regard the conflict as internecine and the issues as eternal. God must be wholly on our side and on none other, and the struggle must be to the death, since if we do not win, and God

found, and it was vanquished once for all by the historic Christ in the wilderness of Judah and on the Cross of Calvary, than in the position of philosophical mysticism that the language of time and sense when applied to these things is vain, and that there never was or shall be true evil in the world at all.

This theoretical shortcoming on the part of mysticism leads to a corresponding practical defect. Monism is of necessity sterile in morals, and wherever mysticism is weak it is weak most of all in the conscience and the will. It does not exercise the soul on its ethical side to the same degree as on the emotional, intellectual, or imaginative side· This may be seen, for example, in the lives of Blake and Coleridge, both excellent mystics, whose characters on the whole were undisciplined and feeble. They may stand for a large class of people of the Bohemian type, to be found especially among the votaries of the arts, whose æsthetic and imaginative sensibilities are highly developed, but who cultivate religiosity rather than religion. These soar readily on the wings of high-flown sentiment and rapture into the region of the supersensuous and the divine, and they as easily flounder back again into the morass of weakness and irresolution. It is a characteristic tendency of pantheistic thought or the unregulated artistic temperament. With the surrender of dualism goes the practical surrender of guilt and responsibility on the one hand, and of grace and personality on the other, and the disappearance of these leads to a weak will and the inevitable relaxing of moral effort. The pleasures of divine enthusiasm are sought by some easier and swifter route than by the long and dusty pathway of obedience, godliness, and self-control. "The Upper Room is reached by a back stair."[1]

The supreme test of all religious systems is their ethical product. "By their fruits ye shall know them," and the fruits of mysticism are not always ripe or overabundant. Mysticism on its weak side tends to moral laziness and spiritual torpor and a kind of holy indifference to action, and an insensibility to the sins and sorrows of mankind. The soul flees thankfully to its pavilion from the strife of tongues, and soars to blissful seats above the press and hurry of external action, where life's perplexing cares and distractions may be forgot. The difficulty is to induce it to return to the travailing world again, in order to reform it and preserve it from dissolution. To the extent to which he thus secludes himself the mystic misses an acquaintance with just so much of divine reality as

[1] See Rufus M. Jones, *Studies in Mystical Religion*, p. xxxvi.

an energetic dealing with the world alone can give. For the salt requires the meat and the yeast the flour, and all feeling that does not express itself in action is apt to lose its vitality and become sickly and sentimental. Some mystics have been nothing more nor less than spiritual epicures, with an exquisitely delicate palate for the good things of God, yet profoundly self-indulgent nevertheless. They have cultivated their godward sympathies at the expense of their manward sympathies, and have thought to become *so* united to God as to leave all poor sinners in the mire.[1] Mystics are in danger of being deceived by the idea that God is more readily to be received into the soul passively than actively. They would rather swoon into the infinite than heal a broken heart, or help a lame dog over a stile. Some might even be counted on, in the manner of the Emperor Nero, to hearken complacently to the music of their own sweet violin while

[1] "And when the soul is thus set aloft, estranged from the fellowship of worldly lovers, though his body be in the midst among them, full far is he parted from carnal affections of creatures. He careth not though he never see man, nor speak with him, nor have comfort from him, that he might for ever continue in that spiritual feeling. . . . And that it may better keep this loneliness, the soul fleeth the [company of all men as much as it can; and seeketh loneliness of body, which helpeth much to the loneliness of the soul, and to the free working of love, the less hindrance that it hath from without of vain janglings." (Walter Hilton, *The Scale of Perfection*, Part III. chap. x.)

the world was burning, or to pursue their heavenly meditations, like Archimedes, amid the crash of all things. It is so much sweeter and more pleasant to build tabernacles on the mount, and to hold rapt converse with Jesus and Moses and Elias, than to have dealings with sordid demoniacs on the vulgar plain. But the true Christianity demands that we be *obedient* to such heavenly visions. If they are to be healthily continued to us they must be accompanied by some courageous plunging into the actual needs, problems, and difficulties of the concrete outer world.

Mystics have always shown a tendency to esteem the contemplative life as pre-eminently divine, and to scorn the merely active life as gross and earthly by comparison. There is doubtless some philosophical justification for this attitude. God Himself, as Absolute Being and Pure Intellect, is necessarily raised far above the dull travail and striving of our morality, He is over all, blessed for evermore. The qualities which we call virtues, such as honour, prudence, courage, temperance, and the like, arise out of the conditions of our earthly life. They must necessarily be inapplicable to Him who from everlasting cannot but contemplate His own perfections. In proportion, therefore, as the soul rises to the divine life and loses itself in God, these lower activities must more and more cease, and the faculties of the higher reason come into play, by which especially we have kinship with God in His self-existent and eternal blessedness. As Dante poetically expresses it, Leah gathering flowers for her own adornment is inferior to Rachel sitting before the mirror and gazing into the depth of her own beauteous eyes, even as she in her turn is inferior to Beatrice, who beholds in ecstatic rapture the transfigured glory of the Christ.

There can be no objection to this mode of conceiving the soul's spiritual ascent, provided the earlier stages of virtuous activity are always faithfully passed through as a preliminary to the later. The error lies in claiming that a life of merely contemplative and exalted feeling is in itself essentially superior to one of moral action.[1] Whereas Christ was content to descend that He might afterwards ascend to heavenly glory, and was highly exalted because he had stooped to become a servant, these mystics think only to ascend and never to descend to life's sores and ministries at all. From the point of view of the beyond, where the soul sings, the humdrum sweat of ordinary morality

---

[1] " As the sensible world is the shadow of the intelligible, so is action a shadow of contemplation, suited to weak-minded persons." (Plotinus, *Ennead*, III. viii. 4.)

seems insufferably dull, insipid, and uninspiring.[1] This way madness lies, and a widely-opened door to the innumerable hallucinations in which pathological mysticism abounds. In such moods as these the fumes of melancholy, the fancies of fanaticism, the whims of caprice, the frenzies of hysteria, and the wildest extravagances of auto-suggestion come to be regarded, without further questioning, as the veritable inspirations of God's own Spirit.

Mysticism, when consistent with itself, is not a propagandist faith. It has little of what the evangelical calls "a passion for souls." Instead of proclaiming aloud from the housetops that which it has heard in the secret place, it rather bids its devotees see that they tell no man the things they have seen and heard. We should do with the divine mysteries, it maintains, what Mary did with the things that were spoken to her by the shepherds, keep them and ponder them in the heart. Why should we throw pearls before swine, or give that which is holy to the dogs? Would they not turn and rend us? What is the use of giving strong meat to babes, or of speaking of the mysteries of

[1] "Virtues, I take leave of you for evermore. . . . Forsooth I wot well your service is too travaillous. Sometime I laid my heart in you without any dissevering. . . . Oh, I was then your servant : but now I am delivered out of your thralldom." ("The Mirror of Simple Souls," *Fortnightly Review*, February 1911.)

the kingdom save to the initiated? Are we not likely to be laughed at for our pains? A Methodist once made the remark, after hearing Emerson preach, that "it would take as many sermons like that to convert a human soul as it would take quarts of skim milk to make a man drunk."[1] The answer that Emerson might well have made would be that he had no wish to convert any human soul, for it was perishing anyway, or else couldn't perish, it mattered little which. In any case the truths which the mystic knows simply cannot be communicated to the multitude. These lack the organs necessary to receive them, and would not, could not, believe, though a revealing angel were sent to them from the dead.

Similarly, the mystic proper is seldom fired by a great and fervent passion for social progress. He moves in a circle of ideas remote from those of secular advancement and evolution. Were the kingdom of heaven to be conceived as a kind of earthly millennium, some day to be realized as a close to the mundane process, it might be worth

---

[1] *Letters of George Birkbeck Hill* (ed. L. Crump), p. 182. Compare Hill's own remark, "How much greater light has been thrown on the world by the invention of lucifer matches, than by the discovery that 'there exists but one being, the Ego, the Absolute!' How much rubbish has the mighty Darwin swept away!" (*Letters*, p. 205.)

while toiling to bring it near.   But the true golden age is no more to be sought in the future than in the past, he believes, and it certainly never will be set up on earth at all.   Rather, heaven lies about us just where we are.   The kingdom of God, being not meat and drink but righteousness, peace, joy in the Holy Ghost, is a realm of values, and is within us and among us even now.   Either it is already attainable here on this world " which is the world of all of us—the place where in the end we find our happiness, or not at all,"[1] or else it awaits us in the Eternal Order.   In any case, we are kept out of it not so much by time or space as by self-will.   Where the goal to be sought is the eternal rather than the final, the way by which we must seek it will be vertical rather than horizontal, to be traversed by prayer rather than by social progress or reform ; and it would not be a whit nearer than it is now, if every man sat under his own vine and fig-tree, and had three acres and a cow into the bargain.   For mysticism the shining goal of humanity is to be found nowhere on this earth, however perfected, and at no point in the long course of time, however, distant.   It looks forward to no cataclysmically introduced millennium at the end of history, no Messianic kingdom or earthly paradise, no final

[1] Wordsworth, *French Revolution.*

guarantee that it represents faithfully some trans-subjective truth, still less some truth that is vital and essential to all religion. The revelations of the Spirit, like those of scripture, are not intended to be given for merely private interpretation. If they are to commend themselves to all men they must be such as can pass both rational and moral tests, and conform to some more impersonal objective standard of truth than mere private feeling is able to supply. In a word, Jesus surely means that even the inner light should be such as can be set upon a lamp-stand and give light to all that are in the house. It is the weakness of mysticism that its truths are seldom capable of being embodied in some statement or institution, and so proclaimed abroad to all the world. Hence its inadequacy to the work of revolutions or great crises of reformation, though it may herald their approach. Mysticism, too, is ill adapted to the organizing of religion on a large public scale, for states and nations. Nor can it publish it successfully among the masses, or impress men where forms and institutions, ritual and ceremony, are required. By virtue of its privacy, its subjective and contemplative nature, it tends to develop into quietism and to become, as with the Quakers, the religion of a cult or select few, the faith of an educated and refined coterie, whose influence is nevertheless out of all proportion to their numbers. Only when a faith has become crystallized into creeds or embodied in institutions can it be translated, as in Catholicism and Evangelical Protestantism, into a propagandist religion for all mankind. The advantage in home and foreign fields of missionary service will always remain with a religion that may truly be described as a gospel, a bringer of good news, and that can proclaim to the sin-stained, the sorrowful, and the wandering, not that something *is*, but that something *has been done*.

Yet, with all its weaknesses and disadvantages, mysticism brings an emphasis which we sorely need, and are beginning to appreciate. Our age is coming to be weary of the false and conflicting claims to authority so strenuously and bewilderingly put forth in favour of Pope, or Book, or Council, and longs for a faith that will bear its authority on its brow. Stress is being laid more and more on the element of personal experience in religion, on inward verities and values rather than on the mere dogmas, however authorized, which have come to us from the past. It is not to be supposed that we shall ever be able to do without dogma, but mysticism has this attraction about it that it provides something in which the soul can rest during the process of theological readjustment necessitated by the advance of Biblical Criticism and the discoveries of science. On all sides things seem to be taking a mystical direction. Science is becoming less materialistic and more spiritual in its conception of matter. Philosophy is ready to admit and even to demand that, however the different systems of human thought may be worked out from first principles, those first principles themselves must be mystically apprehended and assumed. Psychology is feeling afresh the mystery of personality. It is giving an ever larger place to the unconscious and to the subconscious, and is coming to recognize that within the soul's vague borderland are dim vast modes of being yet to be explored. Ethics is becoming more social and less individualistic. Philosophy is recovering from an acute temporary attack of pragmatism, with its over-emphasis on the function of the will in life. There is a general tendency to disparage the rationalizing intellect as an organon for the discovery of the highest truth, and feeling and intuition are coming to their own again. On the whole these tendencies are to be welcomed as likely to carry us in the right direction. We are in dire need of that general heightening and deepening of the religious life which only mysticism can give. So long as we retain the full personality and holiness of God, together with the responsibility and free will of man, and so long as we keep a firm check on the modern tendency to throw off the yoke of what is objective, positive, and dogmatic in religion, in order to give rein to what is merely inward and temperamental and impressionistic, we cannot have too much mysticism.   It is the spring and fountain-head of all our higher life, and wells up within us in every clear call of duty, every instinctive prayer, every unselfish friendship, and every spontaneous act of goodness or pure love.   Purged of its vagaries and nebulosities, the message of mysticism is one of unconquerable optimism and heavenly peace.   It brings with it, where it comes, vision, unworldliness, purity of heart, loftiness of spirit, and the flame of love.   Let but the Church cast this molten metal into fit and proper moulds of effective organization and clear thought, and the world will be won.   There never was a time when there was less prospect of a unity of Christendom on the basis of outward uniformity either of polity or of creed.   Yet never, surely, were men of all possible varieties of faith and worship more ready than now to come together on the basis of sympathetic feeling, and the need of co-operation in urgent practical service.   " Is thy heart right," inquired Jehu of Jehonadab,[1] when they met in the one common enterprise of extirpating idolatry, " as my

---

[1] 2 Kings x. 15.

CONCLUDING SURVEY

IN the course of the present study we have found it most convenient to confine ourselves to English Protestant Christianity subsequent to the Reformation. Previous to that great upheaval all the types of piety found their congenial home within the ample shelter of the Catholic Church. That marvellous organization was an amalgam of all the influences of the past, and inherited the stern ethical dualism of the Jews, the mystical speculation of the Greeks, and the proud objective authority and imperious disciplinary rule of the Romans. For hundreds of years these elements sufficed, and the one Mother Church had breasts for all her sons. But already, at the close of the sixteenth century, children of a more independent life were struggling in her womb, and in the travail of the Reformation they sprang to birth, to pursue thenceforth a vigorous and independent career of their own. The Church of England, at the dawn of the Reformation, was still in all essential respects the old historic Church, and the prevailing type of piety continued to be the sacerdotal. Authoritative dogma, priestly mediation, sacramental grace were generally accepted without question, and the old familiar dualisms of church and world, soul and body, God and nature were unbrokenly perpetuated. But the great religious principle of the anatomy of faith was already being released, and the succeeding centuries were to be devoted to working out the implications which it contained. The human spirit was to discover and affirm its right to free unmediated access to God the Father, with all the far-reaching consequences, religious, philosophical, political, social, and economic, which were to follow in its train.

During the seventeenth century in England, religious men were locked in theological and civil strife. It was an age of great controversies, hot passions, and contending ideals, to be defended and attacked with might and main, both in the study and on the battlefield. Such an age could not but be friendly to the exercise of piety, and all types flourished during this period. The monarchical pretensions of the Stuarts and the assertion of the divine right of kings favoured the sacerdotal type of piety, which is well represented by Hooker, Laud, Andrewes, Herbert, John Donne, and Nicholas

of revolt. Cordially disliking both mystical and evangelical enthusiasm on the one hand, and as fervently resenting the pretensions of sacerdotalism on the other, the Englishman of the eighteenth century made up his mind to settle down quietly to a period of safe religious moderation and respectability and repose. From the dim lantern of the Church, and the glow-worm of the inner light, and even from the divine lamp of the Word of God, so blown on by contending gusts, he was ready to turn gladly to that candle of the Lord which he thought burned ever steadily in the reasoning powers of man. Henceforth that must be the light upon his path. Many influences combined to bring about this result. The founding of the Royal Society and the spread of the scientific spirit gave a great impetus to latitudinarian opinion. Jacobitism during this period was greatly weakened, and with it the belief in the divine right of both kings and bishops. A faint echo of these enthusiasms survived among the Nonjurors, but it became impossible for any one to take a monarchical view of the Church during the reigns of the early Georges. The High Church type of piety, therefore, declined in the eighteenth century, though it was well sustained by Ken and Nelson, and later by Samuel Johnson and Bishop Wilson.

The evangelical was in even a worse plight, and languished woefully till Wesley came. Of the mystical type the most outstanding representative was William Law, who appears almost alone in the century as the advocate of a religion to be apprehended by the heart rather than by the head.

The eighteenth century, on the whole, was an age of reason in religion, and therefore of lukewarmness in devotion. Sanity rather than saintliness was the coveted and ruling virtue, and piety of a sentimental kind was encouraged, and might be fashionable, provided it abhorred "enthusiasm," and was becoming in a gentleman. It was an age in which the Bishop of London, Dr. Trapp, could preach eloquently and most acceptably to a large congregation on "The Great Folly and Danger of being Righteous Overmuch," and Dr. South launch all his thunderbolts "Against Long Extemporary Prayers." The typical publications of the century were Toland's *Christianity not Mysterious*, Tyndal's *Christianity as Old as Creation*, Butler's *Analogy of Religion to the Constitution and Course of Nature*, Paley's *Evidences of Christianity*, and Pope's *Universal Prayer*, in most of which there was nothing distinctive of Christianity at all, and the gospel of the redeeming grace of the Lord Christ was diluted and reduced to the universal findings of the human consciousness. It is not to be inferred from this that deism was incapable of producing admirable Christians. The placid theistic cheerfulness of Addison, Locke, and Newton is singularly attractive,[1] and provided that restrained reasonable religion which the age required, and which we find even in a good deal of the verse of Isaac Watts. But in the end it proved unsatisfactory. The point of view of naturalism chills everything. You cannot get the flame of an ecstatic piety out of the damp wood and leaves of a rationalizing system. "The religious instinct is like an invisible lamp which illumines the inmost recesses of our personality. Bring it to the surface, and it will be extinguished in the crude light of ratiocination, as the stars pale in the glaring light of the sun."[2] The belief that Christianity is a right doctrine which has been evolved from beneath can never produce the same results as the belief that it is a divine rescue and revelation vouchsafed us from above. Philosophically, deism found its historical development in the positivism of Mill and Bentham.

[1] "Benson the Presbyterian told Lardner that he had made a pilgrimage to Locke's grave, and could hardly help crying, ' Sancte Johannis, ora pro nobis.'" (Abbey and Overton, *English Church in the Eighteenth Century*, ed. 1887, p. 105.)

[2] C. Sarolea, *Cardinal Newman*, p. 167.

Spiritually, it led to the reaction of the Methodist revival, and so provided evangelicalism with an opportunity to do its work. With Wesley and his preachers the long drought passed. The windows of heaven were opened to the appeal of prayer, the rains came, and the pastures of the wilderness were refreshed. A characteristic feature of the evangelical movement was the accompanying outburst of lyric fervour in the hymn-writing of Watts, Doddridge, Cowper, and the two Wesleys. Finally, the mystical type of piety received a fresh accession of strength, towards the end of this period, from German Romanticism, and the century closed in a sunset of exceeding glory, with flashings of spiritual radiance from Blake, from Wordsworth, and from Coleridge.

When we come to the nineteenth century we find ourselves in an age of rapidly increasing wealth and material prosperity, such as is not on the whole favourable to piety, save by way of reaction. The first of all the types to show signs of vigorous life during this period was the sacerdotal. It was the aim of the Tractarian Movement of the early 'thirties, with Keble, Pusey, and Newman at its head, to stem the rising flood of liberalism in Church and State, and to substitute for the vapid evangelicalism of the day something more dignified, catholic, and apostolic. War was thereby declared against all English Philistinism, stodginess, ugliness, and latitudinarianism ; churches were furbished up and fair robes woven; the Ante-Nicene Fathers were fetched from dusty shelves and edited afresh ; and the long-neglected trumpet of sacerdotalism was made to sound once more a loud and stirring blast. These things provoked a corresponding revival of the evangelical type of piety, and in the religious awakening associated with the names of Moody and Sankey and Henry Drummond it secured widespread and enduring blessings for the country as a whole. As for mysticism, it fared badly during the nineteenth century, save as it found occasional expression in a few prophetic or poetic souls, such as Thomas Carlyle, Charles Kingsley, Alfred Tennyson, and Robert Browning.

With the results of this rapid historical survey in our minds we may proceed briefly to inquire which type of piety seems on the whole most congenial to our genius as a people. Strictly speaking, there should be no such thing as nationalism in Christian piety, for in Christ there is neither Jew nor Gentile, Barbarian nor Scythian, bond nor free. Yet Christianity has always, in its progress through the world, assumed well-marked features characteristic of the race to which it has brought the

blessings of the gospel, and to this rule English
Christianity has been no exception. In the main
we have developed a straightforward, manly, Teutonic type. English piety has had little of the
fine chivalry and heroism of the mediæval French
type, as we see it in St. Louis or Joan of Arc. It
lacks the deep inwardness which marks the best
German types, with their racial leaning to the
speculative, the mystical, and the profound.[1] We
are unsympathetic also towards the almost fierce
passion of spiritual absorption in God which ran
in the Spanish blood of St. Theresa, or the spirit
of sweet childlikeness and joyous humility which
so well accorded with the sunny Italian nature of
St. Francis of Assisi. Religion, with us, takes an
active rather than a passive form. It appears most
typically in such men as Alfred, Thomas à Becket,
Cromwell, Johnson, Wesley, Bright, Kingsley,
Gladstone, General Gordon, men who have com-

---

[1] " The difficulty of really naturalizing German hymns arises, I
think, less from the mere interposition of a foreign medium of
expression, than from a fundamental difference of national feeling
in the region of religion ; the extreme inwardness of the German
Christian sentiment appearing to us a little sickly and unreal ; and
the more descriptive or historical hymns of our own country seeming to Germans often painfully anthropomorphic, and usually de-
ficient in close personal appropriation of the life and death of the
Redeemer." (Upton and Drummond, *Life and Letters of James
Martineau*, vol. i. p. 345.)

bined fervent piety and heavenly-mindedness with simplicity, manliness, valour, self-reliance, and power to deal effectively with the affairs of this world. It is significant that the patron saint of England is no monk or anchorite, but a resolute and manly warrior, rescuing oppressed innocence from the clutch of violence and wrong.

Mysticism in England has been a plant of tender growth. It flourished with us before the Reformation in Richard Rolle, in Walter Hilton, and in Juliana of Norwich. Since then it has been more or less of an exotic. William Law tried to naturalize it among us by transplanting it from Boehme, Coleridge from Fichte, William Blake from Swedenborg, but never with complete success. So far from being mystical in his religious temperament the Englishman is usually severely practical, when he is not sentimental. He can on occasion show himself a confirmed idealist, but in the main he would rather rest his faith on some acknowledged fact of history or well-established institution than commit it to the clouds of his own fancies. To evangelicalism and sacerdotalism he gives a free hand, bidding them contend for and express the truth that is in them, while approving the extravagances of neither. There is a marked strain of Puritanism in the Englishman's character, as the Stuart kings discovered to their cost. But let the attempt be made by Scottish Presbyterians or others to make him wholly or even mainly Puritan, and he will resent it. Especially is he averse to anything in evangelicalism that savours of cant, humbug, hypocrisy, or deceit.

On the other hand, our typical English piety has generally shown a strong dislike of Rome. "If there are two things on earth which John Bull hates," wrote W. E. Gladstone to the Italian patriot Panizzi, "they are an abstract proposition and the Pope."[1] There may be something political in this, or even geographical. Our strong religious feelings, as well as our other feelings, have often been markedly insular, and we seem to be almost constitutionally incapable of absorbing either institutions or ideas which are properly cosmopolitan. But our instinctive aversion from Rome is not wholly political or historically reminiscent. It is partly racial, a healthy man's rejection of too much frippery, arrogance, subtlety, and superstition in religion. By no one, perhaps, has this feeling been better expressed than by Newman himself in his

[1] Morley's *Life of Gladstone*, vol. i. p. 299. See also a letter to Archdeacon Manning (1850) in which he says that "if the Roman system is incapable of being powerfully modified in spirit, I am convinced it never can be the instrument of the work of God among us ; the fault and the virtues of England are alike against it." (D. C. Lathbury, *Gladstone's Letters on Church and Religion*, vol. i. p. 104.)

16

pre-Roman days. "We Englishmen," he wrote, "like manliness, openness, consistency, truth. Rome will never gain us, till she learns these virtues, and uses them ; and then she may gain us, but it will be by ceasing to be what we now mean by Rome, by having a right, not to 'have dominion over our faith,' but to gain and possess our affections in the bonds of the gospel. Till she ceases to be what she practically is, a union is impossible between her and England."[1]

The bent of the Englishman's genius is towards the practical and seemly in matters of religion. He loves decency and order and comprehension. Let but a religion be sensible and well conducted ; let it be one you can observe with dignity and self-respect ; above all, let it work well and contribute something valuable towards the common good ; and few Englishmen will care to oppose it on purely theoretical grounds, or to trouble much about its theological credentials or historical descent. Our national temperament in this respect is admirably reflected in a letter which Edward Fitzgerald once wrote to his friend Carlyle.[2] "If the old creed was commendably effective in the Generals and Counsellors of two hundred years ago, I think we may well be content to let it still work among the ploughmen

---

[1] J. H. Newman, *Apologia*, ed. 1878, p. 126.
[2] Quoted by A. C. Benson, *Edward Fitzgerald*, p. 186.

and weavers of to-day; and even to suffer some
absurdities in the Form if the Spirit does well on
the whole.   Even poor Exeter Hall ought, I think,
to be borne with; it is at least better than this
wretched Oxford business.   When I was in Dorset-
shire some weeks ago, and saw chancels done up in
sky-blue and gold, with niches, candles, an *Altar*,
rails to keep off the laity, and the parson (like your
Reverend Mr. Hitch) *intoning* with his back to the
people, I thought the Exeter Hall cry of 'The
Bible—the whole Bible—and nothing but the Bible'
a good cry.   I wanted Oliver and his dragoons to
march in and put an end to it all.   Yet your
Established Parsons (when quiet and in their senses)
make good country gentlemen and magistrates ; and
I am glad to secure one man of means and education
in each parish of England.   The people can always
resort to Bunyan, Baxter, and Wesley, if they want
stronger food than the old Liturgy and the orthodox
Discourse." [1]

Each of the types, then, which we have been
studying, can show elements of strength, as well as
peculiar elements of weakness.   The sacerdotal is
the most successful in satisfying the needs of the
sensuous imagination, and by its infinitely varied use
of symbol, ceremony, and suggestion it exercises a

[1] Note S.

magic sway over both mind and heart. It is also much the strongest in historical appeal. Ancient, dignified, aristocratic, with the wisdom of many centuries graven on its brow, it conserves with unerring wisdom what is precious in the past, looks with quiet patience on the hasty novelties of the present, and awaits with surest confidence the conquest of the future. These things make sacerdotalism unapproachable in all solemn pageants and public functions, where pomp and ceremony are required. Its skill, too, in enlisting the services of all the arts in worship, and in making its appeal through symbols which each may interpret privately according to its need, give sacerdotalism a strong hold over minds that have the instinct of true reverence, yet cannot subscribe to the theological formulæ of evangelicalism nor find rest in the vague inwardness of mysticism.

Its weakness is that it is apt to become proud, rigid, exclusive, reactionary, and somnolescent, confining the divine operations to narrowly prescribed channels, wedded to conservatism and the established order, the champion of rank, ancestry, and effete authority, and the foe to new movements of spiritual progress, civil and religious freedom, social, industrial, and political reform.[1] It also tends to be remote

[1] Note T.

from the vital interests and aspirations of humanity, to be blind to the presence of God in ordinary life, and to tithe mint and cummin to the neglect of weightier matters of the law.   The emphasis comes to be placed on forms and ceremonies, and virtue is made to consist in busy externalism and a drone of liturgies.   By these means the soul's enthusiasm and faith are chilled into decorum, the spirit of simple obedience and love to Jesus Christ sinks beneath a weight of elaborate and fussy ritual, a jungle of observances hinders the heart's eagerness to come to the living God, and the religious sense evaporates in a paltriness of chrisms, genuflexions, and gabbled prayers.   This is to render Christ's yoke difficult, His burden heavy, and His commandments grievous. Religion, instead of being made wings to a man, becomes a millstone.   The fatigued soul cannot sustain it.   Sacerdotalism, because of its tendency to attach too much importance in worship to what is non-moral and merely ceremonial and institutional, is thus a sure breeder of scepticism and irreligion.[1]

The glory of evangelicalism lies in its simplicity, its spiritual sublimity, its emphasis on the directness and autonomy of faith, its radical and thorough handling of the soul's direst problems of sin and guilt.   Evangelicalism, like the angel in the Gospels,

[1] Note U.

is a troubler of the waters.   More than other types
of piety it cripples and condemns human nature, sets
it in its utter weakness and unworthiness before a
holy God, and refuses it the comfort of trust in
a rite or compliance with an institution, requiring
from it nothing less than a new birth from above,
and the absolute self-commitment of the total soul
to a crucified Redeemer.   But out of the troubled
waters come wondrous gifts of healing.   Evangelicalism offers the maimed soul a complete, unpurchasable,
immediate, and unmediated deliverance through
Jesus Christ.   It both bids and enables it straightway to arise, take up its bed, and walk ; and then
moves it joyfully to proclaim its salvation aloud to
all the world.   Starting from this centre, evangelicalism proceeds to philanthropic schemes of progress,
and so becomes the forerunner of social and political
reform.[1]

The weakness of this type of piety is on its corporate and institutional side.   The emphasis which
it lays on the faith of the individual, as well as its
extreme diversity of organization, render it unaccus-
tomed to deal effectively and on a large scale with

[1] " Evangelicals and Nonconformists are still the backbone of
serious religion in England. . . . If ever the full power of religion
is to be brought to bear on the masses of the people, these are the
men who will have to do it." (Professor H. M. Gwatkin, *The
Knowledge of God*, vol. ii. p. 246.)

problems affecting the government and authority of the one visible Church, and its relation to the wider life of society and the State. Its proneness, also, to exalt the grace of God sometimes leads it unduly to disparage human nature, even to the point of abjectness and hypocrisy, and to encourage an exaggerated sense of our native sinfulness.[1] The same almost unrelieved stress on the moral aspect of things frequently causes it to be indifferent, if not hostile, to the humanizing influences of culture, and to seem but the sorriest Philistinism in the eyes of those who above all else in religion desiderate sweetness and light and charm. Evangelicalism is well suited to times of religious deadness, apathy, and stagnation ; and it comes forward appropriately with its spiritual quickening when missions and revivals are required. It is not so well adapted to periods of stability and repose, when the need is for a more ordered, elaborate, and stately worship. It accommodates itself but

---

[1] The following quotation from a well-known writer will show how intense, and yet perfectly sincere, the modern evangelical consciousness of sin may be. " Our guilt is so great that we dare not think of it. It crushes our minds with a perfect stupor of horror, when for a moment we try to imagine a day of judgment when we shall be judged for all the deeds we have done in the body. Heart-beat after heart-beat, breath after breath, hour after hour, day after day, year after year, and all full of sin ; all nothing but sin from our mother's womb to our grave." (Alexander Whyte, D.D., *Bunyan Characters*, vol. iii. p. 136.)

little to human nature in the matter of sensuous imagery and appeal, and is poor in those aids to devotion which sacerdotalism so plentifully provides for the sluggish soul in rite, ceremony, and symbol.

The advantage of mysticism, as a form of piety, is that it guards and cherishes those experiences of the soul which by their very nature can neither be formulated into dogmas nor crystallized into institutions.[1]   The service it renders to the Church is to counteract formalism, and to provide for every age the only irrefragable proof of the existence and love of God.   It saves men from all narrowness and sectarianism and sterile utilitarianism; shows them bright gleamings of the divine in what might else be considered common and unclean; and provides a satisfactory basis for Christian faith, in times of fresh criticism or research, when the old beams of tradition are giving way.   Its weakness is that it blurs the Christian outline, and empties the historical revelation of its positive content.   Mysticism tends to degenerate from a faith to a religiosity. It is apt to become a philosophy and cease to be a gospel.   The speculative and emotional elements within it easily overpower the moral.   The result is

---

[1] "Explain it how we may, there would seem to be something transient and incapable of passing into *institutions* in the higher action of God's Spirit in history." (Upton and Drummond, *Life and Letters of James Martineau*, vol. i. p. 431.)

an over-facile optimism and a superficial diagnosis of human sin. And when sin ceases to be understood in its true nature, ethics evaporate, the missionary spirit flags, and a cult remains suited only to the temperaments of a few. Mysticism, while valuable as a spirit suffusing all the Churches, is itself incapable of sustaining an independent Church life, for it readily rejects sacraments and symbols, has little historic sense, and lacks a true understanding of the corporate and institutional character of the Church. It tends to reduce Christianity either to an esoteric secret known only to the initiated, or else to that universal reason which there is no need to communicate or proclaim abroad, since its light already shineth in every human heart.

The characteristics of each type, as above analysed, will naturally determine very largely the particular social classes to which they will severally appeal. Speaking generally, we may say that the sacerdotal type exercises its predominating influence either among the rich or the very poor.[1] Its whole system

[1] Chiefly the former, in the case of the Church of England, according to S. T. Coleridge. " The fatal error into which the peculiar character of the English Reformation threw our Church, has borne bitter fruit ever since—I mean that of its clinging to court and state, instead of cultivating the people. The Church ought to be a mediator between the people and the government, between the poor and the rich. As it is, I fear the Church has let the hearts of the common people be stolen from it. . . . For a long

is congenial to the outlook of those who are either accustomed to rule or are accustomed to obey. An independent democracy is naturally repugnant to it. Evangelicalism, on the other hand, and especially Nonconformity, while they have won their devotees from all ranks, have always flourished chiefly among the middle classes. When ejected from the cathedrals and parish churches, Nonconformity found a congenial home in places like Salters' Hall, Plumbers' Hall, Merchants' Hall, and the King's Weigh-House, there to receive a warm welcome from England's rising prosperity and sturdy strength. A spirit of pushful vigour and enterprise and self-reliance naturally accords well with the evangelical appeal. Hence the widespread influence of this type of piety in large industrial centres. Mysticism, on the whole, makes no appeal to the masses. Its genius is to be the religion of the refined and cultured few, who leave the main stream of national religious life to resort to quiet eddies of spiritual communion apart. Indeed, it would seem that no form of piety can attract the masses that does not deal largely in bold symbolism and suggestion, and support its appeal by the evidence of brotherliness

time past the Church of England seems to me to have been blighted with prudence, as it is called. I wish with all my heart we had a little zealous imprudence." (S. T. Coleridge, *Table Talk*, 8th September 1830.)

and good works.   General Booth has been successful here, and Prebendary Carlisle, both of whom have adopted much the same methods.   But in efforts of this kind it is the personality rather than the method that always counts.   " The working man seldom feels at home in a church with a highly ornate ritual in which he takes little part.   If he does attend, it is because he approves of the Socialistic leanings of the parson, and finds in him a real friend and brother. . . . Men like Mr. Osborne Jay and the late Father Dolling could always attract a fair number of worshippers, because they put the man before the priest." [1]

As for the various temperaments to which the types naturally conform, it may be said that, where this is the chiefly determining factor, the twice-born, the independent, people of a strong and passionate nature, in whom conscience predominates, and an acute sense of man's inability to perform God's commands or make any amends by ceremonies and good works, will gravitate to the evangelical type of piety.   People in whom intuition and vague contemplative feeling predominate will be attracted to mysticism.   The artistic, the methodical, the systematic, those who crave discipline and order, and

---

[1] Percy Alden, in *The Religious Life of London*, edited by Mudie Smith, pp. 37, 40.

who love definiteness, outward authority, and a relief from the perplexities of personal decision in religion, will find themselves most at home with the sacerdotal type. It would be a mistake, no doubt, to suppose that spiritual affinities are determined by temperament alone, for there is a great variety of appeal in all the types. At the same time, strongly marked temperamental characteristics do tend to gather into well-defined groups. We speak of the Nonconformist conscience, for example, and we associate Unitarianism with the cultivation of the intellect. In Roman Catholic worship we are conscious of a special appeal to the sensuous and æsthetic imagination; in Quaker worship, to the spiritual imagination. Where revivals and " gospel " services predominate, the appeal is to the emotions and the will. One type of man demands what is unique, startling, and supernatural to assist his piety; another distrusts everything that is not abstract, natural, and universal. One approaches God best by means of vague reverie, another must draw nigh accompanied by a precise ritual. One man places the whole of virtue in some form of abstinence, another conceives it to consist in the service of the State. One man leans to authority in religion, and must have the support of some external guide; another waits only on his δαίμων, and can hear the clear tones of God's voice nowhere but in the secret admonitions of his own heart. In each case we shall have a distinctly differentiated type of piety, and Laud will not be Fox, nor Fox be Cromwell. Wesley begins as a sacerdotalist, tries mysticism, but abjures it and ends in evangelicalism. Newman, on the other hand, cannot remain in evangelicalism, but wanders till he becomes mystic and sacerdotalist in one. In either case the strong bent of the nature determines the career.

There is one type of piety which has not yet been discussed in these pages, namely, that which prevails among the advocates of what may be best described as liberal Christianity. These cannot take the sacerdotal view of religion, for they regard the sacraments as stimuli and aids to the religious life, rather than as in any sense necessary to it. Still less can they adopt the standpoint of evangelicalism. They do not accept its doctrines, and cannot speak its language of sin and grace. Their affinities are rather with the mystical type of piety, with which they are nevertheless not in close sympathy, because of its tendency to exalt mere subjective feeling over intellect in religion. Liberal Christians, who are to be found in all Churches, naturally seek a rational basis for their belief, and they incline to rest their faith on a simple theism.

There can be no doubt that this type is capable of producing men of the greatest moral elevation and even holiness of life. The sincere, disinterested search for perfect truth may well become the fountain of a most reverent and childlike piety. Gladstone once characterized John Stuart Mill as "the saint of rationalism,"[1] and it would be impossible to name a more saintly Englishman than James Martineau, or read a more devotional book than his *Endeavours after the Christian Life.* Yet the prevalence of intellectualism in this type is somewhat unfriendly to the cultivation of an intensely spiritual ardour. The function of thought in religion is subordinate to that of faith, which apprehends divine objects that may not be rationally grasped, by means of immediate intuition. Where, therefore, reason stands critic over faith, the soul is apt to hesitate and question where it should adore. " Unitarianism," wrote Martineau once, "is scrupulous of the veracities, but afraid of the fervours of devotion."[2] This would seem to be a weakness observable in liberal Christianity as a whole. It is unwilling to admit to the heart what has not first of all been fully sanctioned by the

[1] See Höffding's *History of Philosophy* (Eng. trans.), vol. ii. p. 405.

[2] Quoted by John Watson, D.D., *Hibbert Journal*, January 1903.

brain, and is mortally afraid of too much prostration in devotion.

When members of the group crave spiritual satisfactions which their own intellectualism is scarcely able to provide, they frequently turn sympathetically to one of the other types. Thus Martineau frankly confessed that the springs of his own most fervent piety were non-Unitarian, and that doctrines which he repudiated intellectually had yet a strong hold upon his religious feelings. "Both conviction and feeling keep me close to the poetry and piety of Christendom. It is my native air, and no other can I breathe. . . . The hymns of the Wesleys, the Prayers of the Friends, the meditations of Law and Tauler have a quickening and elevating power which I rarely feel in books on our Unitarian shelves. Yet I can less than ever appreciate or even intellectually excuse any distinctive article of the Trinitarian scheme of salvation."[1] Others have been drawn to a sacramental Church, because of its liturgical and devotional appeal, although they have had but little sympathy with its doctrines. "Inability to adopt the creeds of Christendom," wrote T. H. Green, "in their natural sense—and in any other sense they are best left alone—need

[1] Upton and Drummond, *Life and Letters of James Martineau*, vol. ii. pp. 22, 229.

not disqualify us from using its prayers. . . . In prayer we need not ask whether our words are such as would be understood by others in the same sense as by us, or whether they convey a correct theological conception. They are not meant to be heard of men. 'He that searcheth the hearts knoweth what is the mind of the spirit.' . . . The fact that others who use such prayers have beliefs as to historical occurrences which we do not share, need not prevent us from sharing with them what is not the expression of an historical belief, but of a spiritual aspiration." [1]

On the whole, it may be said that the services of liberal Christianity to the Church are less in the direction of piety than in that of religious thinking. There is need in every age of those who shall advance truth, resist obscurantism, and correct credulity and superstition. Their function is to disentangle from the outworn theology of a past age its essential and vital elements, in order to restate them for the present and the future, as part of our ordered and assured knowledge. Such must try the spirits whether they be of God. It is

[1] T. H. Green, *Works*, vol. iii. p. 274. Similarly, J. H. Short-house argued that an agnostic should be a communicant of the Church of England, because of the sacramental element in things, however he might reject her dogmas. See his *Life*, by his Wife, vol. i. p. 151.

is, God is with us "; and Hooker passes from this world "meditating the number and nature of the angels, and their blessed obedience and order, without which peace could not be in heaven, and oh! that it might be so on earth!" Antinomianism is to be met with in all the types, and where some loophole into laxity of morals is desired, the sacerdotalist can find it in the efficacy of the sacraments, just as easily as the evangelical can find it in justification by faith, or the mystic in the plea of the soul's spiritual detachment from the doings of the body. Nor has any one type the monopoly of narrowness. The bigotry which denies salvation to the unbaptized is brother to the fanaticism which confines it to the elect, or which would exclusively reserve it for the mystically initiated. On the other hand, every type can show fruit of righteousness and good works. Men who entertain the most diverse views on the theoretical aspects of Christianity, and who could not agree as to modes of worship, may yet be undistinguishable when it is a question of a kind action. Find out who is the model employer in your neighbourhood, and he is as likely to be a Quaker as he is to be a Churchman, just as the most satisfactory workman in his employment may prove to be a Catholic, or a Wesleyan, or a Unitarian. Goodness

at all like James or Andrew. And all through
the Church's history there has been a glorious
variety in the characteristics of the saints. We are
thankful for St. Francis, who walked with childlike
wonder in a child's world, who saw with unsophisti-
cated soul the love of God the Father in birds,
in sunshine, and in flowers, and who tasted, as
for the first time, the unspeakable refreshment and
delight which are ever to be found in obedience,
humility, and love, the primal things of life which
all may have. We are thankful also for her, Joan
of Arc, the steadfast warrior maid, who sprang into
the saddle at the call of God, and waved her
country on to faith, to courage, and to hope. No
less thankful are we for Thomas à Kempis, who
draws us to his nook with his little book, and there
lays bare to us the secrets of a heart which is both
his and ours; as well as for R. W. Dale, who takes
us out of the cloister into the street again, and
shows us how the saint should conduct himself amid
the bustle and the din of a great city. How
manifold they are, and what evidence do they give
of the variegated grace of God! In Lawrence,
Havelock, and Gordon we see the saint as soldier;
in Howard, Müller, and Barnardo, the saint as
philanthropist; in Cromwell, Bright, and Gladstone,
the saint as statesman; in Livingstone and Henry

all of them it may be said that they have rendered peculiar and needed service to the Church of Christ. Mysticism has been ever ready to check the barrenness of sacerdotalism and the bigotry of evangelicalism, and keep the soul in warm and sympathetic touch with the living Spirit of God. Evangelicalism has done the needed work of counteracting the torpor of sacerdotalism and the vagueness of mysticism, by presenting a clear and free gospel, and by advancing the religion of Jesus from age to age and from one country to another. The services of sacerdotalism have been to conserve and formulate the gains of both mysticism and evangelicalism and to embody them in institutions suited to the necessities of society and the cravings of the heart. The misfortune begins when, like the disciples of old, the types quarrel with one another, and contend which of them is the greatest and should have the place at Christ's right hand in the kingdom of heaven. The sacerdotalist is in error when he stones the prophet. The evangelical is in error when he libels or vilifies the priest. The mystic is in error when he sets his private impulse against and above the collective testimony of the Church. It is the glory of the Christian religion that it embraces and can utilize all the types, and so make its appeal to men of all kindreds and of every tongue. It rejects no aspect of the truth, however it may seem to be opposed to some other aspect, and has a sheltering wing for whatever is good and right in priest and prophet, in dreamer and doer, in deism and pantheism, in monism and dualism too. This comprehensiveness of spirit arises out of deep inner genius of the religion itself. "Christianity is an ethics of redemption," says a distinguished thinker of to-day, "with a conception of the world both optimistic and pessimistic, both transcendental and immanental, and an apprehension both of severe antagonism and of close interior union between the world and God. It is, in principle, a dualism, and yet a dualism which is ever in process of dissolution by faith and action. It is a purely religious ethic, which concentrates man's soul, with abrupt exclusiveness, upon the values of the interior life; and yet, again, it is a humane ethic, busy with the moulding and transforming of nature, and through love bring about an eventual reconciliation with it. At one time the one, at another time the other, of these poles is prominent; but neither of them may be completely absent, if the Christian outlook is to be maintained. And yet the original germ of the whole vast growth and movement ever remains an intensely, abruptly transcendental ethic, and can never simply pass

over into a purely immanental ethic. The gospel
ever remains, with all possible clearness and keen-
ness, a promise of redemption, leading us away
from this world, from nature and from sin, from
earthly sorrow and earthly error, on and on to
God; and which cannot allow the last word to be
spoken in this life."[1]

There is little prospect, at present, of any outward corporate unity in the Christian Church,
although never was the desire for it stronger than
it is to-day. Not yet can the Jerusalem which
is above, and which is the Mother of us all, descend
in holiness and beauty among the inhabitants of
the earth. But if that consummation is ever to be
attained, and if such a visible city of God is ever
to be established, it must be because it is one that
has gates facing every way, so that every genuine
type of Christian experience can bring its glory
into it, as well as respect and make room for the
glory of every other. Judah must not vex Ephraim,
nor Ephraim envy Judah. Each of the types of
piety we have been considering is probably in the
right in so far as it affirms; each is in the wrong
in so far as it denies. Each has justified its existence by the service it has rendered, and by the

[1] Prof. Ernst Troeltsch, quoted by Fr. von Hügel, *The Mystical
Element in Religion*, vol. ii. pp. 359, 360.

truth it holds in trust. Each has to be supplemented and held in check by the other two; for each, if cultivated exclusively and alone, would soon become false to the truth and would tend to destroy itself. In one another and in God they must learn harmoniously to live. It would be wrong, therefore, to bring about an understanding between them by premature or hasty compromise. If reunion come not now, yet it will come,—the readiness is all. The vision is for an appointed time, and if it tarry we must wait for it. Meanwhile it is for every type of Christian experience to be faithful to the truth for which it stands; to respect, as it would be respected, the complementary truths which others hold; to respond meekly and readily to the drawings of the one Holy Spirit, wherever they may lead; and to pray without ceasing for the peace of Jerusalem and the unity of Zion.

We rise from our study of the subject with an ever-increasing wonder at the glory of the Christ, who is the goal of all the types, and who transcends them all. What is one-sided in each finds its full and perfect complement in Him who is at once the High Priest of our profession, the bringer of our redemption, and the indwelling Spirit who abides in those who love Him, as they in Him, even

NOTES

(*A*) " I have looked over Hutton, Vives, Erasmus, Scaliger, Salmasius, Casaubon, and many other critical grammarians, and all Gruter's critical volumes. . . . I much value the method and sobriety of Aquinas, the subtlety of Scotus and Ockham, the plainness of Durandus, the solidity of Arminiensis, the profundity of Bradwardine; of Aureolus, Capreolus, Bannes, Alvarez, etc. ; of Mayro, Lychetus, Trombeta, Faber, Meurisse, Rada, etc. ; of Ruiz, Pennathes, Saurez, Vasquez, etc. ; of Hurtado, of Albertino, of Lud à Dola, and many others. But how loth should I be to take such sauce for my food, and such recreations for my business! The jingling of too much and false philosophy among them often drowns the noise of Aaron's bells. I feel myself much better in Herbert's *Temple*." (Richard Baxter, quoted in Sir J. Stephen's *Essays in Ecclesiastical Biography*, p. 362.)

(*B*) " If the Divine Being be conceived by us, however vaguely, as holiness and love, and if, independently of rewards and punishments, and without reference to the conditions under which He has made all the blessings of this life (except likeness to Himself) accessible to us, we are inspired by love of Him because of His holiness and love, so that our hearts are unquiet till they rest in conscious communion with Him, then within us there is a devout as distinguished from a virtuous life, for then we seek harmonious relations not only with our social and material environment, but also with our supreme spiritual environment, the ultimate reality." (P. H. Wickstead, *Studies in Theology*, p. 153.)

(*C*) "The English national temperament deeply enjoys the unbroken order and traditions of its Church; the liturgy, ceremony, architecture; the sober grace, the good company, the connection with the throne, with history, which adorn it. And whilst it endears itself thus to men of more taste than activity, the stability of the English nation is passionately enlisted to its support from its inextricable connection with the cause of public order, with politics, and with the funds." (Emerson, *English Traits*, chap. xiii.)

(*D*) The attractiveness of ecclesiastical symbolism is thus quaintly set forth in an old book of the time of Henry the Eighth. "What shall I say of the Gospel when it is sung? Oh, how goodly ceremonies are then done! There is borne a banner of silk and garnished with a goodly cross, in token of the victorious and blessed triumph which Jesus Christ made of subduing the world unto Himself by the doctrine of the Gospel. Then afterwards a priest beareth a censer of silver, making a fumigation and savour of incense, as long as the Gospel is in reading, to signify our inward affection for Christ. There is also borne about the Gospel-book richly covered with gold and silver garnished with precious stones. Afterwards there thundereth a great bell, by which we signify our Christian priestly and apostolical office; last of all the Gospel is borne about to every person in the Quire, and offered forth to be kissed." (*The Old and the New*, quoted by H. M. Luckock, *The Divine Liturgy*, p. 110.)

(*E*) "Of all diseases I have ever hated a palsy in

religion; well knowing, that too often a dead palsy ends that disease, in the fearful forgetfulness of God and His judgments. Ever since I came in place, I laboured nothing more, than that the external public worship of God (too much slighted in most parts of this kingdom) might be preserved, and that with as much decency and uniformity as might be; being still of opinion, that unity cannot long continue in the Church, where uniformity is shut out at the church-door. And I evidently saw, that the public neglect of God's service in the outward face of it, and the nasty lying of many places dedicated to that service, had almost cast a damp upon the true and inward worship of God; which while we live in the body, needs external helps, and all little enough to keep it in any vigour." (Archbishop Laud's *Diary*, March 12, 1643.) Compare "the dreary and unlovely, narrow and unjust monotony of Evangelicalism." (Fr. von Hügel, *The Mystical Element in Religion*, vol. i. p. 10.) "I never knew what worship was, as an objective fact, till I entered the Catholic Church, and was partaker in its offices of devotion. . . . Protestantism is the dreariest of possible religions. The thought of the Anglican service makes me shiver, and the thought of the Thirty-nine Articles makes me shudder . . . a ritual dashed upon the ground, trodden on and broken piecemeal; prayers clipped, pieced, shuffled about at pleasure until the meaning of the composition perished . . . vestments chucked off, lights quenched, jewels stolen, the pomp and circumstance of worship annihilated; a dreariness which could be felt and which seemed the token of an uninspired Socinianism pouring itself upon the eye, the ear, the nostril of the worshipper." (J. H.

Newman, quoted in his *Life*, by Wilfrid Ward, vol. i. pp. 140, 204, 581.)

(*F*) " The Anglican Revival doubted the presence of God in humanity, the activity and reality of His grace outside the limits of a constituted Church, and apart from sacramental persons, instruments, and symbols. It doubted the sanity of the reason He had given, thought that this reason had so little affinity with its Maker as to be ever tending away from Him, its bent by nature being away from God rather than to God. It thus made man an atheist by nature, and so confined divine influence to artificial and ordained channels as to make the common life, which most needs to be illumined and ennobled by the divine, either vacant of God, or alien from Him." (A. M. Fairbairn, *Catholicism, Roman and Anglican*, p. 37.) Compare also the strong language of Milton, " For we have learned that the scornful term of laic, the consecrating of temples, carpets, and tablecloths, the railing in of a repugnant and contradictive Mount Sinai in the gospel, as if the touch of a lay-christian, who is nevertheless God's living temple, could profane dead judaisms, the exclusion of Christ's people from the offices of holy discipline through the pride of usurping clergy, causes the rest to have an unworthy and abject opinion of themselves, to approach to holy duties with a slavish fear, and to unholy doings with a familiar boldness. For seeing such a wide and terrible distance between religious things and themselves, and that in respect of a wooden table, and the perimeter of holy ground above it, a flagon pot, and a linen corporal, the priest esteems their layships unhallowed and unclean, they fear religion with such fear as loves not, and think the

purity of the gospel too pure for them, and that any
uncleanness is more suitable to their unconsecrated
estate." (Milton, *The Reason of Church Government
Urged against Prelaty.*)

(*G*) "There are two parts of our nature essential to
our first approaches to God : imagination places Him
before us as an object of conception external to the
mind : conscience interprets His personal relations of
communion with ourselves. The first of these emphati-
cally needs a mediator. The function of the second
perishes the moment he appears. Jesus Christ, the
centre of the scattered moral possibilities of history, is
thus mediator to our imagination between God and
man. On the other hand, we *cannot allow* the
conscience to resign for an instant its native right of
immediate contact and audience with God : to delegate
the privilege is treason : to quit His eye is death."
(James Martineau, in *Life*, by J. Drummond and C. B.
Upton, vol. i. p. 199.)

(*H*) "The father's will [The New Testament] was
very precise, and it was the main precept in it, with
the greatest penalties annexed, not to add to or to
diminish from the coats [the Gospel] one thread,
without a positive command in the will. Now, the
coats the father left them [the Churches] were, it is
true, of very good cloth, and besides so neatly sewn,
you would swear they were all of one piece ; but at the
same time very plain, with little or no ornament. But
it happened, before they were a month in town
shoulder knots [became the fashion] . . . bars of gold
lace, . . . a pretty sort of flame-coloured satin for
linings, . . . silver fringes, etc." (Swift, *Tale of a
Tub*, §§ ii. and iv.) " They began to draw down all the

divine intercourse betwixt God and the soul, yea, the very shape of God Himself, into an exterior and bodily form, urgently pretending a necessity and obligement of joining the body in a formal reverence, and worship circumscribed; they hallowed it, they fumed it, they sprinkled it, they bedecked it, not in robes of pure innocency, but of pure linen, with other deformed and fantastic dresses, in palls and mitres, gold, and gewgaws fetched from Aaron's old wardrobe, or the flamen's vestry; then was the priest set to con his motions and his postures, his liturgies and his lurries, till the soul by this means of overbodying herself, given up justly to fleshly delights, bated her wing apace downward: and finding the ease she had from her visible and sensuous colleague, the body, in performance of religious duties, her pinions now broken, and flagging, shifted off from herself the labour of high soaring any more, forgot her heavenly flight, and left the dull and droiling carcase to plod on in the old road, and drudging trade of outward conformity." (Milton, *Reformation in England*.)

(*I*) "The doctrine of justification by faith, which diverts the wandering mind from all painful and perplexing retrospect, concentrates the imagination on one Sacred Figure, and persuades the sinner that the sins of a life have in a moment been effaced, has enabled thousands to encounter death with perfect calm, or even with vivid joy, and has consoled innumerable mourners at a time when all the commonplaces of philosophy would seem but the idlest of sounds. It is impossible to say how largely it has contributed to mitigate some of the most acute forms of human misery." (W. E. H. Lecky, *History of England*, vol. ii. p. 639.)

(*J*) " The Nonconformist spirit is, in succinct summary, the spirit which exalts life above organization. More than that, it is the spirit which holds that life should *make* organization, and that organization is at least greatly reduced in value (sometimes even valueless, sometimes actually harmful), unless it be thus the direct product of life. . . . With one school of thought — the Conformist, the more distinctly ecclesiastical — it is with organization that thought about the matter begins; the organization is looked upon as the power-house, the manufactory in which the forces which make the life reside and out of which they issue; so that the primary duty of the religious man is to conform himself to, to become a member of, the organization, in order that he may obtain the needed action upon life. . . . The Nonconformist spirit begins, not with an organization which is held to be the one necessary for the production of life, but further down and further back. Whatever organization comes into existence must be the already existing life weaving for itself an outward and visible dress. . . . The primary duty of the religious man, on this view, is not to conform to whatever religious organization he finds already occupying the field, but to secure for himself the presence and energizing power of a religious life, and thereafter to let that work itself out into an organization which shall be at the same time the life's product and the life's new inspiration." (H. W. Clark, *History of English Nonconformity*, vol. i. pp. 3, 4.)

(*K*) " The precious spark of liberty had been kindled and was preserved by the Puritans alone; and it was to this sect (whose principles appear so frivolous and whose habits so ridiculous) that the English owe the whole freedom of their constitution." (D. Hume, *History of England*, chap. xl.) "Not to the Church of England, nor to Scottish Presbyterianism, nor to English Puritanism at large does the honour of the first perception of the full principle of Liberty of Conscience, and its first assertion in English speech, belong. That honour has to be assigned, I believe, to the Independents in general, and to the Baptists in particular." (D. Masson, *Life of Milton*, vol. iii. p. 99.) "When I look back to the history of this country, and consider its present condition, I must say that all that the people possess of liberty has come, not through the portals of the cathedrals and the parish churches, but from the conventicles, which are despised by hon. Gentlemen opposite." (*Speeches by John Bright, M.P.*, ed. Rogers, vol. i. p. 301.) "It is by the sects, including the Independents, that the English added to what was done by Luther and Calvin, and advanced beyond the sixteenth century ideas. . . . The Independents fought, as they expressed it, not for their religion, but for liberty of conscience, which is the birthright of man." (Lord Acton, *Lectures on Modern History*, pp. 200, 201.)

(*L*) It is true that the S.P.C.K. (1699) and the S.P.G. (1701) had been founded long before the Evangelical Revival, through the zeal, not of evangelicals only, but of the whole Church, laymen especially taking a leading part. But these societies were never missionary in the modern sense of the term. They aimed primarily at educating the poor, circulating good literature in the army and navy, and promoting religion generally throughout the British Empire. It was their supineness and antagonism to all evangelical effort at the close of the eighteenth century that compelled the formation of the quite new societies referred to in the text. See G. R. Balleine, *History of the Evangelical Party in the Church of England*, p. 181.

(M) See E. Gosse, *Father and Son*, pp. 322, 337, and Shelley's reference, in the *Letter to Maria Gisborne*, to

> "those in philanthropic council met,
> Who thought to pay some interest for the debt
> They owed to Jesus Christ for their salvation,
> By giving a faint foretaste of damnation
> To Shakespeare, Sidney, Spenser, and the rest
> Who made our land an island of the blest."

(N) "A kind of waking trance I have often had, quite from boyhood, when I have been all alone. This has generally come to me through repeating my own name two or three times to myself silently, till all at once, out of the intensity of the consciousness of individuality, the individual itself seemed to dissolve and fade away into boundless being; and this not a confused state, but the clearest of the clearest, and the surest of the surest, the weirdest of the weirdest, utterly beyond words, where death was an almost laughable possibility, the loss of personality (if so it were) seeming no extinction, but the only true life." (*Life of Tennyson*, by his Son, vol. i. p. 320.)

(O) "In the attempts to cultivate and support religious meditation of the higher type, the ritualist has often appeared more psychological in his devices than did the Puritan of old, who endeavoured to support religious life by excluding what he regarded as a confusing or as a corrupting appeal to the senses. In so far as the devices of exclusion, which so often characterize the Puritan forms of worship, were accompanied by an equal fear both of externally attractive sense experiences, and of many of the forms of worship which mystics have employed for the sake of arousing the fitting organic sensations, Puritanism, in some of its forms, seems to have tended inevitably to the impoverishment of religious experience. When it escaped this result, and passed through its times of awakening and of fervour, its success was due not to its mere exclusion of appeals to the senses, but to its encouragement of those forms of sensory experience which were connected with strenuous and dutiful activities, and with motor processes accompanying earnest prayer." (J. Royce, *Outlines of Psychology*, p. 128.)

(*P*) "The great mysticism is the belief which is becoming every day stronger with me that all symmetrical natural objects, aye, and perhaps all forms, colours, and scents which show organization or arrangement, are types of some spiritual truth or existence, of a grade between the symbolical and the mystic type. When I walk the fields I am oppressed every now and then with an innate feeling that everything I see has a meaning, if I could but understand it. . . . Oh! how I have prayed to have the mystery unfolded, at least hereafter. To see, if but for a moment the whole harmony of the great system! To hear once the music which the whole universe makes as it performs His bidding! Oh, that heaven! The thought of the first glance of the Creation from thence, when we shall know even as we are known!" (*Charles Kingsley: His Letters and Memories of his Life*, by his Wife, ed. 1895, p. 28.)

(*Q*) "Thou hast lost *Jesus*, but where? Soothly in thy house, that is to say, in thy soul. Nevertheless,

other Oriental faiths, was contrary to the genius of the Teutonic race, with its independence, its self-will, its free life, and its contentiousness. Hence the Teutonic races, in which these Aryan characteristics are the most strongly developed, were the last to submit to the yoke of the Gospel. Now that Christianity has spread over Europe, it is divided into two opposing camps, the Catholic and the Protestant, the Church of Authority and the Church of Reason, the line of division coinciding very closely with the line which separates the two great races of Aryan speech. The dolicephalic Teutonic race is Protestant, the brachycephalic Celto-Slavic race is either Roman Catholic or Greek Orthodox. In the first, individuality, wilfulness, self-reliance, independence are strongly developed ; the second is submissive to authority and conservative in its instincts. To the Teutonic races Latin Christianity was never congenial, and they have now converted it into something very different from what it was at first, or from what it became in the hands of the Latin and Greek doctors. The Teutonic peoples are averse to sacerdotalism, and have shaken off priestly guidance, and developed individualism. The German princes . . . the Scandinavians . . . the Lowland Scotch, who are more purely Teutonic than the English, have given the first development to the genius of Protestantism. Those Scotch clans which have clung to the old faith have the smallest admixture of Teutonic blood. Ulster, the most Teutonic province in Ireland, is most firmly Protestant. . . . Where Teutonic blood is purest, in the Lothian, in Yorkshire, in East Anglia, Protestantism has found an easy entrance. . . . The Welsh and Cornish, who became

Protestant by political accident, have transformed
Protestantism into an emotional religion, which has
inner affinities with the emotional faith of Ireland and
Italy. . . . The England which is orthocephalic is
neither Catholic nor Protestant, but Anglican.'' (Isaac
Taylor, *Origin of the Aryans,* p. 247.)

(*T*) " All the great works of Charity in England
have had their beginning out of the Church; for
instance, the abolition of the slave trade and of
slavery, and the persevering protest of the Anti-
Slavery Society. Not a Catholic name, so far as I
know, shared in this. . . . The whole Temperance
movement. It was a Quaker that made F. Matthews
a total abstainer. Catholic Ireland and the Catholics
of England, until now, have done little for Temperance.
The Anglican and Dissenting ministers are far more
numerously total abstainers than our priests. The
Act of Parliament to protect animals from cruelty was
carried by a non-Catholic Irishman. The anti-vivi-
section Act also. Both are derided, to my knowledge,
among Catholics. The Acts to protect children from
cruelty were the work of Dissenters. On these three
Societies there is hardly a Catholic name. . . . I might
go on. There are endless works for the protection of
shop assistants, over-worked railway and train men,
women and children ground down by sweaters, and
driven by starvation wage upon the streets. Not one
of the works on their behalf was started by us; hardly
a Catholic name is to be found in their Reports.''
(Purcell, *Life of Cardinal Manning,* vol. ii. p. 780.)

(*U*) " The Romanist, or semi-Romanist, whose
religion is chiefly a sense of the mysterious, the
solemn, and the awful, and whose flesh creeps when

he sees a miracle in the consecration of the sacraments, ends, as is well known, in infidelity, when enlightenment and reason have struck the ground of false reverence from beneath his feet." (F. W. Robertson, *Sermons,* vol. i. p. 202.) "At best materialistic media can be but imperfect instruments of the spirit; the line of progress will lie more and more in treating them as suggestive symbols, not as possessing intrinsic value or as efficacious in themselves. Sacramentarianism, although it claim a divine sanction, has in reality more affinity with the magic of primitive religion; it is in substance a revival, not a true development, of the religious idea, and does not belong to the origins of Christianity." (G. Galloway, *Principles of Religious Development,* p. 190.) "The sacraments are a child of an age of deep weariness and spiritual twilight. Divine energies were to proceed towards man, but it was imagined that these energies needed sensuous signs which, however, conceived as necessary pledges of the truth of Divine energies, became more than sensuous. In order to hide the contradiction embedded in this, a dim twilight time and a dreamy disposition of life are necessary. The fresher life of modern times has scattered this twilight and has reduced an alleged piety to magic." (R. Eucken, *The Truth of Religion,* Eng. trans., p. 565.)

INDEX

ACTIVE and contemplative life, 218–22.

Acton, Lord, 274.

Andrewes, L., 31–9, 108, 118.

Anglican Church, characteristically English, 15–8, 43, 268; imaginative and historical appeal, 18–20; range of influence, 62, 249.

Anglican Evangelicals, 84.

Anglican worship, beauty of, 18–25, 269.

Antinomianism, 149–51, 258.

Apostolic succession, 12, 83.

Arminianism and Calvinism, 68.

Art and symbolism, 9, 21–4, 48, 131–9, 244, 268.

Atonement, the, 74–5, 167–9.

Authority, in sacerdotalism, 9, 11, 51, 54; in evangelicalism, 88, 89; in mysticism, 170–1.

Baxter, R., 44, 55, 101, 143, 267.

Bible, 34, 86–90, 109–112, 261.

Bigg, C., 61.

Bright, J., 274.

Bunyan, J., 55, 87, 105–19, 126, 135.

Ceremonialism, 63–5, 245.

Church, sacerdotal view of the, 9–15; evangelical view of the, 78–84.

Clark, H. W., 273.

Classes, relation of piety to social, 249–51.

Coleridge, S. T., 42, 189–99, 209, 217, 249.

Collectivism, influence on religion, 152–3.

Conscience, in sacerdotalism, 59–60; in evangelicalism, 90–8, 251, 271; in mysticism, 217–8.

Cowper, W., 119–30, 142.

Cromwell, O., 97, 134.

Democracy, 62, 251.

Dissent, 62.

Emerson, R. W., 62, 223, 268.

English character, as reflected in the Anglican Church, 15–18; influence of evangelicalism on, 90–4; its religious affinities and dislikes, 238–43.

Eucharistic worship, 12, 24–7, 48–9, 196.

Evangelical type of piety, general features, 68–78; conception of the Church, 78–84; in Anglicanism and Nonconformity, 84–6; attachment to the Bible, 86–8; seat of

281

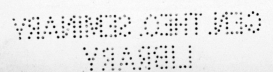